AN INTRODUCTION TO THE HONG KONG LEGAL SYSTEM
THIRD EDITION

An Introduction to the Hong Kong Legal System
Third Edition

Peter Wesley-Smith

HONG KONG
OXFORD UNIVERSITY PRESS
OXFORD NEW YORK
1998

Oxford University Press

Oxford New York
Athens Auckland Bangkok Bogotá
Buenos Aires Calcutta Cape Town Chennai Dar es Salaam
Delhi Florence Hong Kong Istanbul Karachi
Kuala Lumpur Madrid Melbourne
Mexico City Mumbai Nairobi Paris São Paulo Singapore
Taipei Tokyo Toronto Warsaw

and associated companies in
Berlin Ibadan

Oxford is a registered trade mark of Oxford University Press

First published 1988
This impression (lowest digit)
1 3 5 7 9 10 8 6 4 2

All rights reserved. No part of this publication may be reproduced,
stored in a retrieval system, or transmitted, in any form or by any means,
without the prior permission of Oxford University Press.
Within Hong Kong, exceptions are allowed in respect of any fair dealing for the
purpose of research or private study, or criticism or review, as permitted
under the Copyright Ordinance currently in force. Enquiries concerning
reproductions should be sent to
Oxford University Press (China) Ltd at the address below

This book is sold subject to the condition that it shall not, by way
of trade or otherwise, be lent, re-sold, hired out or otherwise circulated
without the publisher's prior consent in any form of binding or cover
other than that in which it is published and without a similar condition
including this condition being imposed on the subsequent purchaser

British Library Cataloguing in Publication Data
available

Library of Congress Cataloging-in-Publication Data
available

ISBN 0-19-590577-6

Printed in Hong Kong
Published by Oxford University Press (China) Ltd
18/F Warwick House, Taikoo Place, 979 King's Road,
Quarry Bay, Hong Kong

This edition is dedicated to
Martin Wesley-Smith

Preface to the Third Edition

THIS edition accommodates changes to the legal system of Hong Kong necessitated by the transition on 1 July 1997 from British to Chinese rule. There have been many other developments to notice as well. The objective of previous editions — to provide a short and inexpensive overview in plain, readable prose — has remained. The law is stated as at April 1998.

PETER WESLEY-SMITH
UNIVERSITY OF HONG KONG
APRIL 1998

Contents

Preface		vii
Glossary		xii
Figures		xiv
1	INTRODUCTION	1
	What Law is Not	1
	What Law Does	3
	Law and Morality	4
	Law and Justice	5
	The Legitimacy of Law	8
	The Transfer of Sovereignty in 1997	9
2	THE LEGAL SYSTEM: AN OVERVIEW	12
	A Legal System	12
	Rules and Principles and Other Precepts	12
	Processes	13
	Institutions	13
	Personnel	15
	Ideology	15
	Classifications of Law	18
	Sources of Law	19
3	THE CONSTITUTION	20
	Types of Constitution	20
	Hong Kong's Written, Concrete Constitution	21
	Hong Kong's Abstract (Broad) Constitution	21
	The Ideology of the Constitution	23
	Simple Characteristics of the Constitution	24
4	THE GOVERNMENT	26
	Gubernatorial Government	27
	The Executive Council	30
	The Public Service	31
	The Legislative Council	32
	Municipal and Rural Government	33
	Law-enforcement Agencies	35

5	**IMPORTED LAW**	37
	Common Law and Equity	37
	The Reception of English Law	38
	English Common Law and Equity	40
	Applicability and Modification of Common Law	42
	British Legislation	44
	National Laws	46
6	**LAW MADE IN HONG KONG**	47
	Primary Legislation	47
	Subsidiary Legislation	49
	Common Law and Equity	50
	Chinese Customary Law	50
7	**LITERARY SOURCES OF LAW**	54
	Sources	54
	The Statute Book	55
	Law Reporting	59
	Secondary Materials	63
8	**THE COURTS**	65
	Terminology	65
	Magistracies	67
	The Coroner	68
	The District Court	68
	The Court of First Instance	69
	The Court of Appeal	70
	The Court of Final Appeal	70
	The Small Claims Tribunal	71
	The Labour Tribunal	72
	The Lands Tribunal	72
	Other Tribunals	73
	Appeals	75
9	**THE OPERATION OF DECISIONAL LAW**	76
	Declaring Law or Making It?	76
	Ratio Decidendi and *Obiter Dictum*	79
	The Doctrine of Precedent	83
10	**STATUTES: CREATION AND INTERPRETATION**	87
	The Process of Legislation	87
	Delegated Legislation	90

	Statutory Interpretation: General	91
	Statutory Rules	91
	Common Law Approaches	92
	Presumptions	94
	Other Principles	96
11	LEGAL PERSONNEL	97
	The Chief Executive	97
	Legislators	98
	Legal Officers	99
	Lawyers	100
	Judges and Magistrates	105
	Justices of the Peace	110
	Academics	111
12	OTHER ASPECTS OF THE LEGAL SYSTEM	112
	Juries	112
	Legal Aid, Advice, and Assistance	113
	The Bill of Rights	115
	Law Reform	116
	The Language of the Law	117
	The Ombudsman	118
	The Delivery of Legal Services	119
	Notes	123
	Index	130

Glossary

A.C.	Appeal Cases (like 'Q.B.' [q.v.], the name of a series of *The Law Reports* published by the Incorporated Council of Law Reporting for England and Wales)
App. Cas.	Appeal Cases (a series of law reports preceding 'A.C.' [q.v.])
C.L.J.	*Cambridge Law Journal*
cap.	Chapter (referring to an ordinance with subsidiary legislation found in the Laws of Hong Kong)
ch.	Chapter (of a book; a chapter of the Laws of Hong Kong is abbreviated 'cap.' [q.v.])
Ch.	Chancery (a division of the High Court in England and the name of a series of *The Law Reports*)
Cmnd.	Command (the designation of a series of publications from Her Majesty's Stationery Office)
E.R.	English Reports (a compendium of reprinted private reports of cases from English courts mostly before 1866)
G.N.	Government Notification
H.K.L.J.	*Hong Kong Law Journal* (the principal periodical on local law)
H.K.L.R.	*Hong Kong Law Reports* (printed and headnoted judgments from the former Hong Kong Supreme Court and the Judicial Committee of the Privy Council and now the High Court and the Court of Final Appeal)
L.H.K.	*Laws of Hong Kong* (the statute book)
LLB	Bachelor of Laws
L.Q.R.	*Law Quarterly Review*
L.R.	*Law Review*
p.	Page
Q.B.	Queen's Bench (a division of the High Court in England and the name of one series of *The Law Reports*)
QC	Queen's Counsel (now Senior Counsel)
s.	section (separate provisions of ordinances are called

	sections and are divided into subsections and paragraphs)
W.L.R.	*Weekly Law Reports* (like A.C., Ch. and Q.B. [q.v.], published by the Incorporated Council of Law Reporting for England and Wales)

Figures

5.1	How to Determine Whether a Decisional Rule is Part of HKSAR Law	45
6.1	Legal Sources of Hong Kong Law	52
7.1	An Ordinance	57
7.2	A Law Report	61
8.1	Hong Kong Courts and Appeals	73
8.2	How to Determine Which Court or Tribunal Ought to Consider a Particular Matter	74

1. Introduction

THIS is a book about the legal system of the Hong Kong Special Administrative Region. Part of the legal system is the law, and in this introductory chapter a few basic and often puzzling questions about the law are examined. An overview of the legal system as a whole is presented in Chapter 2. The rest of the book describes and explains the legal and constitutional framework within which government is currently carried on in Hong Kong. (The present chapter uses terms and concepts which are explained subsequently, and you may find it easier to go straight to Chapter 2 and come back to this one later on.)

WHAT LAW IS NOT

It is usual to begin books of this sort with the question 'What is law?' A definition of what we are to study would certainly seem a good way to start. The answer to the question, however, is invariably: 'Don't know', for there is no orthodox opinion on such a weighty matter, and it would probably be merely confusing to attempt a simplified version of the author's choice amongst the numerous respectable alternatives. It is better to begin by indicating, not what law *is*, but what it *is not*.

The word 'law' is used in several other contexts and its different usages must be distinguished. Our concern is with the law of the legal system, or 'legal law'. This might at first sight seem an unhelpful expression, like 'a fictional novel', but whereas all novels are fiction, not all laws are legal. Legal law is not any of the following:

1. *Physical law* — There are laws of thermodynamics and a law of gravity (what goes up must come down). These are derived from observations of the physical world and are tested by experiments with real objects. They *describe*, whereas legal laws *prescribe*: the latter are normative, telling us what we may or may not do. Physical laws are concerned with cause and effect: they predict what will happen if certain conditions exist, or explain what has already occurred (outside the subatomic sphere, at least). Legal laws

indicate what we *ought* to do in order to avoid punishment or achieve a desire.

2. *Societal or historical law* — Karl Marx propounded laws such as the ever-increasing misery of the working classes under capitalism and the necessary and inevitable triumph of socialism. Parkinson's First Law states that work expands so as to fill the time available for its completion. Parkinson's Second Law is: expenditure rises to meet income. According to Murphy's Law, what *can* go wrong, *will*. These laws are formulated from study of the course of history, or the nature of society, or the characteristics of human endeavour. Again, they tell us what does or will happen, not what *ought* to occur.

3. *Religious law* — The Roman Catholic Church forbids abortion and contraception. Muslims (and Jews) proscribe the eating of pork, Hindus the eating of beef. Moses said: 'Thou shalt not covet thy neighbour's wife.' These laws, directed to those who hold certain religious beliefs, are much closer to legal laws than are physical or societal laws; they are normative, and thus aim to affect people's behaviour. But their origin is divine rather than human, and they apply only to members of the religion concerned. Religious laws, at least in Hong Kong, are not identified with the state or the government. However, it is true that in some countries, for example Iran, there is little real difference between religious and secular legal orders, and in England religious (ecclesiastical) law is also part of the common law.

4. *Moral law* — A rule of behaviour prescribed by ethics, for example fidelity within marriage, is normative, and may be very similar or identical to a legal law in content. (In some states it is a crime to commit adultery.) But a moral rule is to some degree self-imposed, and its infringement does not lead to the kind of regular, organized sanction (punishment) which the apparatus of the legal system may bring to bear on illegal conduct.

5. *Rules of etiquette and fashion* — Should men stand when a woman enters the room or leaves the table? Should skirt hemlines be worn above or below the knee this year? The answers to such questions might be clear and supported by the almost invariable practice of all persons in the community. Yet, as for breach of moral rules, failure to observe such laws brings forth a response quite different from the sanction which follows a criminal act.

From the reasons why legal laws are distinguishable from the laws just mentioned one could construct a series of tests: legal law is normative, laid down by human beings, administered by social institutions, encouraged by organized sanctions, and so on. But these would not be precise or sophisticated enough to amount to a satisfactory definition; too many doubtful cases would be unexplained. You probably know enough, purely intuitively, to recognize that the subject matter of the legal system is not the laws of the physical sciences, sociology, history, religion, morals, etiquette, or fashion. That is sufficient. To go further would plunge us into the depths of legal theory and jurisprudence. Lawyers and judges do not generally know any legal theory or jurisprudence, yet they manage to identify and operate legal laws without much difficulty.

WHAT LAW DOES

Legal laws (this expression will not be used again in this book!) forbid, permit, identify, authorize, empower, declare, oblige, entitle: there are many different forms particular laws can take. It should not be supposed that the 'thou shalt not . . .' model of law is the only one. The main *social functions* which law has can be divided into direct and indirect functions. According to one analysis, there are six social functions (or at least *purposes*) of law:

1. *Law prevents undesirable behaviour and secures desirable behaviour* — We are not free to assault our neighbours or to flood their kitchen by declining to turn off our bathroom taps. Criminal law and the law of tort both prohibit such acts by us and protect us from such acts by others. Individuals in society are thus granted personal security; law and order is established, enabling social and economic life to develop.

2. *Law provides facilities for private arrangements between individuals* — People may make commercial contracts, marry each other, form companies, or join trade unions, thus freely entering into patterns of legal relations which further their interests.

3. *Law provides services and redistributes goods* — Legal arrangements provide for municipal services, taxation, education, the defence of the community against external aggression, and so on.

4. *Law settles disputes* — The operation of courts and tribunals is controlled by laws laying down procedures. Clear law can obviate the need to go to court at all.

5. *Law regulates its own creation and application* — Law refers to itself: legal rules identify other legal rules; determine how they can be created, changed, applied, abrogated, and enforced; and establish institutions for these purposes.

6. *Law communicates and reinforces social values* — Unlike the foregoing, this is an *indirect* social function: a law may be passed to grant a public holiday at Ching Ming, for example, which indirectly permits or encourages the maintenance of a traditional custom. Law can play a symbolic and educative role in society.

All these functions are performed by various techniques: by punishing wrongdoers, providing the remedies and institutions to enforce them, conferring social benefits, raising revenue, and validating private arrangements. One major technique in the modern world is the use of a regulatory system, providing administrative means by which permitted activity is controlled or supervised through licensing or inspection mechanisms.

LAW AND MORALITY

As pointed out above, law and morality are different concepts. Their content may overlap, and in form they are similar, but they are distinguishable in the ways in which they are created and maintained. Yet the relationship between the two is often discussed and often confused.

Some laws might be considered morally valuable, others morally harmful; many laws will have no moral content at all. Society has one set of laws, but many different moralities, even though there may be general agreement on a few basic moral principles. It has not generally been found useful to equate law with morality and thus to declare an immoral law to be invalid. A citizen has a *legal* duty to obey all law, but whether a morally bad law ought in fact to be obeyed depends on one's morality.

The influence of law and morality on each other is considerable. Moral attitudes tend on some matters to be affected by whether the law makes certain conduct illegal. Much criminal law is based on, and reflects, moral ideas; so do such other areas as, traditionally, the law relating to marriage (which in England used to be administered by ecclesiastical or church courts). Chinese law and custom is largely composed of the rules of proper conduct. But should conduct be made illegal simply because it is regarded as immoral where there are no other interests to be protected? This, like the question of obedience to law, is a moral issue. The former law of Hong Kong which made homosexual acts between males a criminal offence was an example of law seeking only to proscribe immoral behaviour. Should it have been liberalized, as the Law Reform Commission of Hong Kong proposed and the legislature finally accepted? A brief discussion of this question illustrates some of the social consequences of law.

Firstly, the anti-homosexuality law was unlikely ever to have prevented homosexual orientation, which is a condition over which an individual has little or no control. It may have deterred some homosexual acts, but certainly not all, and thus the direct social function of the law was limited. Secondly, however, its indirect effects were no doubt widespread and generally unfortunate. A minority group in society was persecuted because of a mere sexual orientation. When the criminal process is mobilized against a homosexual, the distress it causes is considerable. There is a large expenditure of resources in attempting to detect offences which, in their nature, are usually very difficult to detect. The law must be selectively enforced, giving to police officers a broad discretion which is open to abuse. Measures to control AIDS in Hong Kong may well have been inhibited, as homosexuals were liable to police harassment if they revealed their homosexuality. The social harm, therefore, done by a law which could not achieve its primary purpose was extensive and unnecessary.

It is a general principle of the legal system in Hong Kong that we are free to do as we will, provided we do not interfere with the rights of others and there is no law against it. Where others' rights are not involved, the law should be slow to intervene, for the legal prohibition of behaviour reduces our freedom and is capable of causing great suffering. This kind of law is objectionable unless clear advantage to the community is demonstrated. Other kinds of law — those providing facilities or services, for example, or regulating law itself — are not subject to such criticism.

LAW AND JUSTICE

The connection between law and justice is even closer than the connection between law and morality. Justice, however, is a controversial concept, meaning different things to different people. The legal system, nevertheless, promotes a particular style of justice, one which is inherent in many aspects of the law and the way the system is organized. It deserves thorough explanation, for it contrasts with more popular notions and gives rise to much unnecessary dissatisfaction with the law. We are referring here to the justice which is done in the resolution of disputes, by the exercise of the *judicial* function.

The contrast can be illustrated by listing ten pairs of opposing ideas or attributes, as follows:

	Model A	Model B
1	Rule	Discretion
2	A government of laws	A government of persons
3	Reason	Intuition
4	Impartiality	Involvement
5	Generality	Particularity
6	Formal	Informal
7	Abstract	Concrete
8	Order	Revolution
9	Procedure	Substance
10	Law	Equity

The left-hand column (Model A) represents the justice of the common law; the right-hand column (Model B) represents the alternative approach.

The differences between the two sets of terms are stark. The common law system, such as we have in Hong Kong, emphasizes *process* rather than *result* and insists that justice is done when general rules are applied in a formal, impartial fashion. (These rules and principles ought themselves, of course, to be just, in the sense that they are fair and even-handed and likely to produce a result we find satisfying.) The end product is right and proper, or fair, or just, because of the manner in which it has been achieved. Law implies the denial of anything that looks like arbitrariness. Law is indifferent to the outcome; it employs an artificial reason which downgrades the personal preferences of decision-makers and elevates order, regularity, even-handedness, detachment, and neutrality. Justice lies more in the method of proceeding from premise to premise than in the conclusion.

Compare this with the terms listed in the right-hand column. Model B is concerned with achieving a particular result through the exercise of discretion, with satisfying an intuitive sense of justice, if necessary by informal means. Hard and fast rules are denigrated as standing in the way of a desirable resolution of disputes. The important consideration is the present, not the past or the future; it is the satisfying of immediate wants, of finding the merits rather than applying the established rules.

These models are exaggerations, but they serve to demonstrate an important bias of the common law. The Hong Kong system gives prominence to *law* and its measured, careful administration. Thus it proclaims the rule of law as a primary objective (see Chapter 2); it ensures that the law is published and available (Chapter 7); it utilizes the accusatorial or adversarial approach to court proceedings (Chapter 8); it adopts, at least partially, the declaratory theory and the rules of binding precedent (Chapter 9); it limits judicial discretion in the interpretation of statutes (Chapter 10); it requires its judges to have been trained and experienced in the law (Chapter 11); and it seeks to promote access to legal services (Chapter 12). The administration of justice is open to the press and the public, is impartial, and is conducted solemnly according to strict rules of procedure and evidence, with no parties condemned or their interests affected without being given notice and a right to be represented and to be heard. 'Due process' is the ultimate virtue. A system which exemplified the characteristics of Model B would have none of these: justice would depend not on law, but on the sense of rightness of the particular judge. An example is the revolutionary mode of proceeding in China in the early 1950s or during the Cultural Revolution: politics before law; the concrete case before the abstract formal principle.

In practice, no judge can be immune from the attractions of 'doing justice in the instant case', of achieving a result which is intuitively right. There is always a tension between the values espoused in the opposing models, from both sides of the equation. Thus the Chinese system tends to adopt the regular procedures of Model A, and the common law tends to slide towards Model B. The rigour of the common law gave rise to equity (see Chapter 5), which softened the system as a whole; the absolute doctrine of precedent is continually under pressure; juries can, perfectly properly, act in a way which seems perverse (see Chapter 12); and the Chief Executive can remit sentences imposed by the courts (Chapter 4). These represent contradictory impulses, but the main style of justice adopted in Hong Kong is clear: provided the law is properly ascertained and applied according to due process, justice is done. The parties to a dispute may not approve of the result, but they have at least been treated fairly.

THE LEGITIMACY OF LAW

Why (to ask what might seem a curious question) is the law of Hong Kong the law of Hong Kong? Who or what gives it the right to order us about? Why should it govern us, and why should we obey it? The answer to the last question is probably that if we do not, we'll be punished. But most of us accept that the law and the legal system in Hong Kong are in some way *legitimate*: we generally obey the law, not simply because life would otherwise be less pleasant for us, but because we believe it to be right that we should do so.

The claim that the Hong Kong system is legitimate involves at least two ideas: that its institutions and precepts are appropriate or proper, and that there is both a legal and a political (or moral) justification for the exercise of power by the present regime. Officials and ideologues endeavour to persuade the populace that institutional arrangements make for wise government which is responsive to public opinion and conducive to the welfare of the whole community. The doctrine of the rule of law is part of this process of persuasion, and, if accepted, it is a powerful argument in favour of the legitimacy of the system which embodies it. That is the first concept of legitimacy: we appreciate the virtues of legality, and, if those virtues are available in Hong Kong, the system gains our support.

The second concept of legitimacy requires good legal and political reasons before a particular system can be approved. A satisfactory *legal* explanation exists for the constitutional distribution of power in Hong Kong: the National People's Congress (NPC), legislating for a part of its territory, has permitted it. But that explanation depends on one fundamental assumption: that Hong Kong is indeed part of a China legitimately ruled by the NPC and the Chinese Communist Party. From this flows everything else. An official act is lawful if authorized by valid legislation; legislation is valid if made by the proper lawmaker; and the proper lawmaker is identified according to the local constitution laid down by the NPC. Compliance with the rules of the system ensures the legality of behaviour. This is so because the law decrees it. That law is valid because it results from an accepted political situation: China asserted control over Hong Kong, Great Britain voluntarily relinquished sovereignty, and the arrangement was sanctified in the Joint Declaration of 1984, which is a treaty valid in international law; China then established a constitution and a legal system which officials and citizens and other countries acknowledged and relied upon. Without that political fact, the law would have no claim to our respect and allegiance.

At bottom, therefore, law is dependent upon politics. In one sense it is a rationalization of a political event, a transformation of a state of affairs brought about by force into a situation governed by law. The constitution reflects and sustains victory on the field of battle. It is, nevertheless, legitimate, for it is in fact obeyed and accepted as such by most of the Region's inhabitants.

THE TRANSFER OF SOVEREIGNTY IN 1997

The resumption of the exercise of sovereignty over Hong Kong by China in 1997 was a significant event for the legal system. The intention was that the territory's 'way of life' should remain unchanged for 50 years, and in general it could be said that only those aspects of Hong Kong's government and other systems should be altered which were in some way incompatible with the transition from British colony to Chinese special administrative region. The agreement reached with the United Kingdom in the Sino-British Joint Declaration of 1984 has been largely implemented in the Basic Law of the Hong Kong SAR. The Basic Law is the fundamental document upon which the legal system now rests. Its principal provisions, so far as they affect the subject of this book, are as follows:

1. The SAR is authorized to exercise a high degree of autonomy and enjoy executive, legislative, and judicial power, including that of final adjudication (BL2).
2. No law enacted by the SAR legislature shall contravene the Basic Law (BL11); that is, the legal system now has a fundamental law much more extensive and restrictive than under the colonial regime. In a number of areas, such as human rights, the economy, education, science, religion, and social services, provisions are made which determine

SAR policy and otherwise constrain the government's freedom of action. The Basic Law itself cannot be amended except by the NPC (BL159).
3. The SAR shall safeguard the rights and freedoms of SAR residents and others (BL4), and Chapter III of the Basic Law provides a list of 'fundamental rights and duties' which are constitutionally protected. These include equality before the law (BL25), the right to vote and stand for election (BL26), freedom of speech, assembly, association, and demonstration (BL27), freedom from arbitrary or unlawful arrest, detention, imprisonment, search, and deprivation of life (BL29), and the right to confidential legal advice, access to the courts, and to institute legal proceedings against the acts of the government (BL35). In these areas the SAR legislature is unable to deprive residents and others of their rights.
4. The laws previously in force — not including Acts of the United Kingdom Parliament, unless they were part of Hong Kong by virtue of an ordinance — are maintained, except for any that contravene the Basic Law (BL8, 160). Documents, contracts, and rights and obligations, subject to the same proviso, shall continue to be valid and protected by the SAR (BL160). A few ordinances were declared by the Standing Committee of the NPC to contravene the Basic Law and were thus not carried into the SAR period; others were amended to make them fit the new system.
5. The SAR comes directly under the Central People's Government (CPG), though its high degree of autonomy is assured (BL12).
6. Only two major areas of policy are denied to the SAR: foreign affairs and defence (BL13, 14).
7. SAR legislation may in some circumstances be returned and invalidated by the Standing Committee of the NPC (BL17), and national laws may be applied to the Region (BL18).
8. The courts shall have independent judicial power, including that of final adjudication; restrictions on their jurisdiction imposed by the legal system and principles previously in force in Hong Kong are to be maintained, and the courts have no jurisdiction over 'acts of state such

as defence and foreign affairs' (BL19). Ultimate power to interpret the Basic Law resides in the NPC Standing Committee, though the courts are permitted concurrent power of interpretation in most cases (BL158).
9. Certain laws, relating to treason, secession, sedition, subversion, etc, shall be enacted by the SAR on its own (BL23).
10. The institutions of government remain broadly similar to those in the colonial period: the Chief Executive replaces the Governor, the Legislative Council and the Executive Council are redefined but with the same roles and with much the same powers, the court system is reproduced except that the Court of Final Appeal replaces the Judicial Committee of the Privy Council.

On 1 July 1997 the Provisional Legislative Council passed the Hong Kong Reunification Ordinance, which confirmed pre-July bills passed by that body, endorsed the appointment of judges, provided for the interpretation of law previously in force, established courts, dealt with the continuity of the laws previously in force, of legal proceedings, and of the public service, and so on.

The political transition occurred smoothly and largely without incident, though of course there were many controversies and challenges to the wisdom of certain measures. So far as the legal system is concerned, the establishment of the Provisional Legislative Council to replace the legislature elected in 1995 raised doubts, not all of them dispelled by the decision of the Court of Appeal which upheld that body's legality. The relationship between the Basic Law and SAR legislation has yet to be clearly worked out. The meaning of the 'one country, two systems' slogan cannot be known without some years of practical operation. There are other uncertainties, as is to be expected at a time of momentous constitutional change: the broad principles of the new system are understood, but 'the devil is in the details', and many questions remain to be settled. The legal system is thus still in a state of flux.

2. The Legal System: An Overview

A LEGAL SYSTEM

It is not possible to define a legal system with precision. A system can be seen as a body of rules and principles (or precepts, or norms), processes, institutions, and personnel or actors; a legal system is one in which the primary concern of its components is the creation and regulation of law. This definition is not entirely satisfactory for various reasons, but it will suffice for the purposes of this book.

RULES AND PRINCIPLES AND OTHER PRECEPTS

The law is a collection of rules, principles, standards, and concepts whose end is the regulation of human behaviour. Some of these precepts are expressed at a high level of generality, while others are very specific; some prohibit certain forms of conduct, while others provide citizens with the means to satisfy their wants; many directly impinge on the individual, and some refer principally to other rules or principles. All together they make up a coherent whole calculated to facilitate the implementation of social values.

One way of distinguishing between them is to examine their mode of origin. There are two principal ways of making law. The first is by a legislative act creating statute or *enacted* law: rules and principles specifically laid down in accordance with a formal procedure by an institution (a *legislature*) whose privilege of making law is recognized and accepted by the community at large. The primary legislature in Hong Kong is the Legislative Council (BL66, 73), and the law which it enacts, if signed and promulgated by the Chief Executive (BL76), is contained in *ordinances*. Its legislation can probably be overridden by national legislation made in China, and law-making power is subject to various limitations set out in the Basic Law. The Hong Kong legislature can delegate lawmaking powers to other government bodies such as the Chief Executive in the Executive Council. The resulting *delegated* (or *subsidiary*) legislation, comprising rules, regulations, by-laws, and so on, usually supplements ordinances and provides more detailed prescriptions of what citizens may or may not do.

The second main way of formulating legal precepts is through judicial activity, from which emerges *common law* or *decisional law* (or case-law): non-statutory rules and principles formulated and enforced by judges in their day-to-day decisions on the disputes which come before them. These are often called 'judge-made' law, but this begs the question whether judges do in fact 'make' law. Prior to 1997, local judges were generally required to follow the common law of England, though they were enjoined to take into account the particular circumstances of Hong Kong and of its inhabitants. The common law of England remains part of the 'laws previously in force' applying in the SAR. In many areas of human behaviour the legislature has intervened only partially or not at all, and decisional law, which can be abrogated by statute, fills in the gaps which are permitted to remain by legislative inactivity.

Apart from enacted law and decisional law, Chinese custom is a source of legal rules in Hong Kong, but it is now of minor importance for most citizens.

Underlying all three sources are certain fundamental understandings which give coherence to the whole body of legal precepts. The principal classifications of these precepts are considered later in this chapter.

PROCESSES

Law serves no purpose if it remains static: it must be invoked and mobilized and focused on the conduct it is designed to control. The means by which precepts are brought into operation are the processes which get the legal system moving. They enable a citizen to discover what the relevant norms governing his behaviour are; they bring him before a court; they permit him to be punished or give him a remedy against a wrong. Too numerous to be described here, they are crucial to the effectiveness and efficiency of the legal system.

INSTITUTIONS

Legal institutions create law, change it, maintain it, regulate it, interpret it, apply it, and enforce it. They are usually divided into three categories. *Legislative* institutions enact law, as described above; *judicial* institutions are the courts and tribunals whose primary function is to settle disputes amongst citizens and between citizens and the government; *executive* institutions endeavour to protect citizens and develop society in accordance with policy and law.

Traditionally, Hong Kong's legislative institutions have not been controlled by the local populace, and despite some progress towards democratization in the last few years, reform has been slow and piecemeal. The Chief Executive was selected through a voting process involving a tiny minority of Hong Kong citizens and was appointed by the Central People's Government in Beijing; and although the members of the Legislative Council are elected (from May 1998) by Hong Kong citizens, most are indirectly elected or are elected from very small constituencies. It is doubtful whether in practice Hong Kong people have a significant say in choosing the precepts and processes of the system.

Judicial institutions consist of a whole range of courts and tribunals within the territory. The Court of Final Appeal is the ultimate court of appeal for the system, but it is rarely resorted to by Hong Kong litigants; most appeals stop at the Court of Appeal which, with the Court of First Instance, makes up the High Court in Hong Kong. The High Court's jurisdiction is civil and criminal, original and appellate. Its original jurisdiction covers the more serious criminal offences and the civil proceedings with most at stake. An intermediate court is the District Court (civil and criminal jurisdiction), while relatively minor crime is dealt with by magistrates. Coroners deal with death inquiries, the Lands Tribunal adjudicates upon claims for compensation on resumption of land, and the Inland Revenue Board of Review decides taxation matters. With these bodies the procedure is formal and highly stylized, with legal representation permitted and strict rules of evidence followed. The dominant notion is the *accusatorial* or *adversarial* system of trial, the judge sitting as impartial umpire of a contest between two (sometimes more) parties. Rather less expensive, and often much more in accordance with the non-lawyer's sense of justice, is the *inquisitorial* approach where the judge actively participates in determining the true facts and encouraging the parties to settle their differences amicably. Such a style has been partially adopted in the Labour Tribunal, which is the forum for dealing with employment disputes, and the Small Claims Tribunal. In addition to these bodies there are a variety of other more administrative tribunals which determine matters of fact and law.

Executive institutions include the Executive Council, which formulates policy for translation into ordinances by the legislature, the civil service, the police, and the Independent Commission Against Corruption (ICAC). Two government departments which play a particularly important role in the legal system are the Department of Justice and the Legal Aid Department. The former houses various legal officers (including the Secretary for Justice, the Solicitor General, and the Director of Public Prosecutions), and is responsible for law drafting, criminal prosecutions, legal advice to the government, and so on. The latter department is responsible for administering the system of legal aid by which means-tested citizens can be advised and represented in the courts by trained lawyers without charge. Supplementing this department's work are other schemes which provide free legal advice and assistance.

Outside the categories of legislative, judicial, and administrative institutions is the system of legal education which, within the territory, is the monopoly of the University of Hong Kong and the City University. Students enrol for a three-year bachelor of laws degree, followed by a one-year course of vocation-oriented instruction and then apprenticeship to a practising solicitor or barrister. Lawyers from other jurisdictions may take a transfer test to qualify them for private practice in Hong Kong.

PERSONNEL

The main actors in the legal system are legislators, judicial officers and other court officials, government legal officers, police, members of the ICAC, law teachers, litigants, and lawyers in private practice. Like England, Hong Kong has a legal profession which is divided into two branches: solicitors and barristers.

IDEOLOGY

Law's primary role is in relation to human behaviour: law governs citizens' conduct through the norms applied by institutions and personnel in accordance with the system's processes. The ends to be achieved — the type of behaviour required, the private arrangements permitted, the services supplied — depend on the political philosophy and culture of the community whose legal system is being examined. These objectives are, in a sense, outside the system, which is often thought to be a neutral vehicle. But there are certain values which are espoused by the system itself and at least partially reflected in it; they may even be considered inherent in the very concept of a legal system.

These values are expressed in the rather elastic notion of the rule of law, which can be explained in the following overlapping principles:

1. *Law is a formal, rational system* — Legal precepts are self-consistent and generalized, made by persons whose competence to make them is acknowledged, and made in accordance with a regular, open, and stable procedure. They can be ascertained in an objective manner, for all law is published and available and the relationship between different rules and principles is clear. Judges, when selecting rules to apply to cases which come before them, have very little real choice; the law is therefore certain and predictable. The legal order, it can be said, is relatively autonomous from the political order: the reasoning processes it uses, the persons who operate it, the institutions which administer the law, and the law itself, are distinct from and, in a sense, independent of politics.

2. *Law is the antithesis of arbitrary power* — This is perhaps the core principle of the rule of law. Every citizen, including government officials and judges, must obey the law. The legal standards by which conduct is judged are pre-existing: they are precepts which are fixed and announced beforehand. Law should not be retroactive if it imposes burdens, and arbitrary power can be prevented or subsequently condemned by agents (police, lawyers, judiciary) of the legal system. No person, therefore, can be made to suffer, in body or pocket, except for a clear breach of law established in the courts. It is, of course, possible for legislation to give very wide, vague powers to an official and to prevent courts from examining his exercise of them, but this can be condemned as broadly unconstitutional and contrary to the spirit of the rule of law — and in some circumstances might be contrary to the Bill of Rights and the Basic Law.

3. *Everyone is equal before the law* — The law applies equally to all, whatever their social status, rank, class, political influence,

physical strength, wealth, political views, religion, race, nationality, or sex. Justice is blind, it is said, to the differences between individuals; the law is no respecter of persons. Even government officials, legislators, and judges are subject to the general law in the same manner as ordinary citizens.

4. *Law is impartially administered* — Judges, who are chosen solely for their legal expertise, determine facts and apply law in an impartial manner, free from interference of a political or personal nature from any source, including (and in particular) the executive government. They are empowered to review the legality of all behaviour, including the making of law and its execution. Judicial independence is protected by a number of constitutional rules and conventions. The decision whether to institute proceedings for a breach of the law belongs to the Secretary for Justice, who in this respect is legally answerable to no one, though she follows guidelines published by her predecessors which seem to be generally acceptable to the public. Lawyers have a duty to represent citizens regardless of their own views of a person's political beliefs or of his alleged conduct. Access to the legal system — to lawyers and ultimately to the courts — is available to all, and every person is entitled to know what the case is against him, to be heard in answer to the case, and to have his conduct judged by officials who have no self-interest or personal bias. Legal rights and duties are connected to remedies by which aggrieved persons can seek redress for illegal conduct.

5. *Law is capable of guiding behaviour* — Law is general, published, prospective, comprehensible, consistent and coherent, capable of being obeyed, relatively constant, and regularly and fairly administered.

6. *Law is advantageous to the individual* — Law provides a settled framework for social, political, and economic relationships. It promotes order and personal security, respects human dignity and individual autonomy, and ensures formal justice (in the sense explained in Chapter 1).

It must be emphasized that, firstly, there are some exceptions to these principles; they cannot all be absolutely maintained, though deviations from them are always to be regretted and should be as small as possible. Secondly, although the rule of law has been explained in *descriptive* terms, its achievement is a matter of degree. The Hong Kong legal system aspires to, but does not exhibit, the rule of law in its purest form. The rule of law is not 'a rule of law' but a constitutional principle and an objective informing the behaviour of lawyers and judges. It is *prescriptive*, being a set of standards or internal guidelines. Thirdly, some observers doubt that these standards are capable of being achieved at all in a capitalist society or, indeed, that they are desirable, since they may stand in the way of reform to the benefit of all sectors of society. They are part of the *ideology* of the system, serving to persuade citizens that social arrangements are just when in fact they institutionalize injustice (according to Model B notions).

CLASSIFICATIONS OF LAW

There are different ways of classifying legal precepts or norms. We have seen already, and will see again, the categories of enacted law, decisional law, and customary law. They are distinguished by their relative *strength* (statute is superior to — will override if inconsistent with — the others, and it is the judges who decide whether, and the extent to which, customs survive as legal precepts) and by their *mode of origin*.

These enacted, case-law, and customary rules and principles can be distributed into other categories according to the system to which they belong, their geographical origin, the job they do, or the kinds of rights or powers to which they are related. There are separate systems (though they overlap at points) of international law and municipal (or domestic) law. *International law* is primarily concerned with the rules and principles governing the behaviour of independent and sovereign states and of international organizations and institutions. The precepts of the Hong Kong legal system and constitution are not part of this collection: they belong to the realm of *municipal law*, along with all other rules and principles governing the private behaviour of the citizen and his or her relationship to the government. Within this category a distinction can be drawn between national and regional law. *National law* is made in mainland China by the National People's Congress, or its Standing Committee, for China generally or for Hong Kong specifically. Certain laws or resolutions of the NPC fall into this class, including the Basic Law, as well as decisions affecting the transition from British to Chinese rule. Most Hong Kong law is local or '*regional*' law, made in the Hong Kong SAR. (Common law and any surviving English legislation applied to Hong Kong by ordinance can be considered local law.) Applicable national and local law together comprise the whole of municipal law, with the exception of some precepts which owe their origin to international law but which take effect in the municipal legal system.

According to one analysis, rules of law can be considered either *primary* (they directly govern citizens' behaviour) or *secondary* (these refer to primary rules, determining whether they exist, how they are made and changed, and how they are to be applied and enforced). Such a classification is not to be confused with primary legislation, made by a principal legislature like the National People's Congress, and subsidiary legislation such as regulations authorized solely by primary enactment. Some precepts belong to *substantive law* because they affect the substance of a person's powers, rights, duties, liabilities, and so on, while others make up *procedural law*, being concerned with the recognition and enforcement of substantive law. Another categorization is between *public law* (affecting government: constitutional law and administrative law belong here) and *private law* (affecting the relations between individuals, such as the law of contract and tort). *Criminal law* is composed of rules relating to punishable offences against the general public interest, while *civil law* is concerned with the rights and duties of persons and institutions in relation to each other.

Each of these categories can be further classified and subdivided. None can be precisely defined and, being established for different purposes, they tend to overlap. They are necessary, however, if the norms of the legal system are to be clearly identified, ordered, and used to provide a stable and just regime for the exercise of power and the settlement of disputes.

SOURCES OF LAW

It will be pointed out in Chapter 7 that the word 'sources' can have four different meanings. We are concerned in this book with two types of source: *legal* or authoritative sources, indicating the ways in which law is made (legislation, decisional law, and Chinese customary law), and *literary* (and computerized) sources, comprising the written materials from which we can discover what the law is (the statute book and the law reports). Legal sources are discussed in Chapters 5 and 6 and literary sources in Chapter 7.

3. The Constitution

TYPES OF CONSTITUTION

The constitution of a state or territory establishes ('constitutes') the basic institutions of government, distributes governmental authority amongst them, defines the relationship between them, and determines their relationship to individual citizens. Some constitutions are said to be *written* or *codified*, meaning that there is one document (or a small number of documents) which sets out the fundamental rules relating to these matters. Countries like Australia and the United States of America have a written constitution in this sense. A very few other countries, in particular the United Kingdom, have no such document, and constitutional rules and principles have to be culled from a variety of sources: enacted laws, judicial decisions, and established practices or conventions. These rules and principles make up what is called the *unwritten* or *uncodified* constitution.

Another classification distinguishes between a concrete or narrow constitution and an abstract or broad constitution. A *concrete* (narrow) constitution is the document (or documents) which comprises the written constitution: the most basic rules are all together in one place. But not all the precepts relating to the institutions and attributes of government can be easily collected and proclaimed in this concrete fashion. The broad outline can be presented in a concrete, written constitution, but the details and the glosses are worked out in practice when difficulties and disputes arise. Thus particular legislation, or decisions by the courts, contribute to the complex of precepts which fall into the category of constitutional, and all these additional materials are referred to as the *abstract* (broad) constitution. (It should be noted that 'abstract' in this sense does not necessarily mean 'vague', or 'not practical', or 'not ideal'; and 'concrete' means written on paper, not set in a mixture of gravel, sand, and cement!)

The United Kingdom has no written or concrete constitution—its constitution is unwritten and abstract. But Hong Kong, on the other hand, in effect has two constitutions: one which is written and concrete (codified and narrow), because many important rules can be found in it, and a complementary abstract (broad) constitution as well.

HONG KONG'S WRITTEN, CONCRETE CONSTITUTION

Hong Kong is regarded as a special administrative region of the People's Republic of China under Article 31 of the Chinese Constitution. The Basic Law is regarded, at least locally, as the written, concrete (or narrow and codified) constitution of Hong Kong. (Usage in the PRC does not confer 'constitutional' status on the Basic Law, but in the terminology with which Hong Kong lawyers are familiar the Basic Law is undoubtedly a 'constitution', supplying many of the fundamental rules and institutions of government.)

The pivot of the executive and legislative institutions provided for by the present constitution is the office of the Chief Executive. The Chief Executive is the principal executive officer: he is the head of the Region and represents it (BL43), and all government personnel in Hong Kong owe him obedience. In this capacity he is advised by, and is in most circumstances enjoined to consult (BL56), the Executive Council. He signs bills into law (BL76) and may return a bill to the Legislative Council (BL49). The Chief Executive, the Executive Council, and the Legislative Council are the essential institutions of the executive and legislative branches of the Hong Kong government. They have combined to establish the third branch, the courts of justice, which exercise judicial powers.

HONG KONG'S ABSTRACT (BROAD) CONSTITUTION

The Basic Law has constituted the principal executive and legislative bodies and granted them appropriate powers in broad terms. But this constitution is brief and concise, and it cannot, and does not pretend to, elaborate on all the rules and principles affecting the government. These additional precepts are discovered in other sources, and it is the abstract constitution which contains them.

There are several of these sources. Some decisions of the NPC, for instance, are constitutional in nature: an obvious example is the appointment and ratification of the work report of the Preparatory

Committee which provided for establishment of the Provisional Legislative Council in 1997 to 1998. The common law is another source, because it is judges who have traditionally drawn the boundaries between the various branches of government and between government and citizens. The prerogative, in all probability a supplementary source of government power in Hong Kong, is accepted by and defined by the common law, and many of the rights and liberties of Hong Kong citizens owe their origin and maintenance to judges exercising common law powers in the course of settling disputes. Ordinances of the Hong Kong legislature are also capable of laying down constitutional rules, such as those permitting proceedings against the SAR government or indeed regulating governmental institutions like the High Court. Similarly, the practice or custom of the legislative branch, much of which is set out in the Standing Orders of the Legislative Council or in resolutions of that chamber, is constitutional.

Supplementing the enacted or formally declared precepts of the abstract constitution are so-called *conventions*, which are practices or usages considered necessary to the smooth functioning of the government system. They have been described as the flesh which clothes the bare bones of the law. Their importance gives them a special character, and breach of them, while not usually involving conduct which can be pronounced illegal, is regarded as improper and unconstitutional. The theoretically vast powers of the monarch in the United Kingdom are tightly constrained by conventions, and the effectiveness of such broad principles as the rule of law is heavily reliant upon them. Whether there are conventions significantly inhibiting the politics of the SAR is an intriguing question; certainly some will eventually develop, and some have probably been inherited from the pre-1997 regime. Conventions are frustrating things for students of the law, for they are sometimes rather imprecise, but they cannot be ignored if a constitution as an efficacious, functioning phenomenon is to be understood. An example, crucial to the principle of the independence of the judiciary, is the idea that the executive branch of government must not attempt to influence the way judges interpret and apply the law; when civil servants in Hong Kong succumb to the temptation to tell the judiciary how to behave they are roundly and properly criticized.

There are many legal precepts, and perhaps established practices as well, which are constitutional because they affect the distribution or exercise of government authority, but which do not appear in the Basic Law. It is not the narrow, concrete but the broad, abstract constitution which must be consulted in order to discover them.

THE IDEOLOGY OF THE CONSTITUTION

There are certain very general notions which stand behind and inform the more particular rules and principles of the constitution. These can be referred to as the constitution's *ideology*: they comprise a collection of political, philosophical, or moral ideas which have influenced and continue to influence the constitution-givers, the lawmakers, and the opinion-settlers. One result of the transition to Chinese rule is that it may be a long time before one can confidently describe the ideology of the Hong Kong system: the traditional values of the common law are no doubt still relevant, but they are unlikely to be shared in all respects by the Central People's Government and they may be softened or abandoned in the SAR as time passes and the influence of Chinese officials in the territory increases (assuming, of course, that such influence does indeed increase).

One such notion — which, it was suggested in the preceding chapter, is inseparable from the institution of a legal system — is the rule of law. We have already seen that, in its fundamental meaning, this asserts that the law should precede the behaviour to which it is to be applied; only a pre-existing law can, with justice, be used to punish an individual for his or her conduct. Certain subsidiary principles must be recognized if this principle is to be effective, including the equal application of law to all citizens; government by law would soon seem to be arbitrary and unfair and lacking in authority if it did not apply, for example, to the officials who are responsible for it. And if rules exist to protect people from the abuse of government power, they must be capable of being enforced; that is, there must be legal remedies and thus access to an impartial arbitrator in order to secure the predominance of regular law.

As explained in the preceding chapter, it may be misleading to suggest that the rule of law is a useful device when *describing* the constitution of Hong Kong — there are too many necessary exceptions to it and regrettable lapses from it to detect any such idea by studying the actual constitution. It is a guiding principle, an *ideal* incapable of complete realization yet reflected in many constitutional precepts of a more precise kind.

Constitutional lawyers often discuss a general technique for limiting the ability of government officials to wield excessive powers to the detriment of citizens' rights. This is contained in the doctrine of the *separation of powers* (or of *functions*). The three types of power — legislative, executive (or administrative), and judicial — should be distributed amongst three distinct branches of government; no branch should exercise more than one variety of function, and no person should belong to more than one branch. Each branch is balanced by the others, some kind of parity is established between them, and dictatorial powers therefore cannot easily be assumed by one person or a small, cohesive group of persons. This theory has been adopted in various ways in many constitutions, and despite exceptions (for example, a number of executive institutions make delegated legislation), to a large extent it seems to underpin the Basic Law. Certainly the judiciary is required to be independent of the executive branch of government, and judges' freedom to apply the law equally without fear or favour is important to the rule of law and is, indeed, fundamental to the whole constitution.

In addition to the separation of powers, the Hong Kong system exhibits a number of *independent power points* or *nuclei of autonomy*: institutions which exercise authority within the state, but are not regimented by the executive government. The judiciary is the most important of these, but there is also the Secretary for Justice exercising her prosecutorial discretion, the legal profession (in particular the Bar), members of the legislature, and juries answering the question: 'Guilty or not guilty?' So long as these bodies remain independent of political pressures, it is difficult for the administrative authorities to bend the law in their own interests and thus to subvert the rule of law.

SIMPLE CHARACTERISTICS OF THE CONSTITUTION

The constitution of Hong Kong, as described above, is both concrete and abstract, consisting of precepts which are formally enacted by a legislature, or formulated by the judges, or which emerge gradually from the practices and philosophies of people concerned with government. There are other characteristics which can be briefly explained.

Firstly, it is a *controlled* constitution: there are special procedures for changing the rules (BL159): amendment of the Basic Law must be proposed by certain bodies only, be studied by the Committee for the Basic Law, and be compatible with the Joint Declaration. The local legislature cannot amend it. And some constitutional precepts or notions, such as the independence of the judiciary, are so firmly entrenched in constitutional ideology that they comprise what is no doubt in practice a quite inflexible or rigid part of the constitution.

Secondly, it is a *'regional'* constitution: it formally states that Hong Kong is an inalienable part of the People's Republic of China (BL1) of which it is a local administrative region directly under the Central People's Government (BL12). The SAR is nevertheless promised a high degree of autonomy.

Thirdly, while in formal terms the legislative and executive branches of government are distinct, there are links between them. To a limited degree, the executive branch is accountable to or responsible to the Legislative Council, but only in the sense that question time, or debate, or committee may subject the performance of the executive government to scrutiny and criticism. The executive must obey the law which emanates from the legislature, but it is not otherwise subordinate to the lawmaking branch. The Chief Executive is accountable to the Central People's Government as well as to the SAR (BL43) and, being appointed by Beijing, can be dismissed only by Beijing. However, Article 52 of the Basic Law lays down that he must resign if, for example, an intractable Legislative Council opposes him in certain circumstances.

Finally, great importance is attached to the *independence of the judiciary*. Judges are generally independent of the executive branch, and constitutional precepts exist to encourage and preserve their duty to decide in accordance with law rather than with executive policy. The courts enjoy a 'high degree of autonomy' in administering justice. Judges belong to a 'judicial service' distinct from the civil service of government.

4. The Government

THE expression 'the government' means, in the broad sense, the exercise of functions by executive, legislative, and judicial institutions of the state. It thus comprises the Chief Executive, the Executive Council, the civil service, the Legislative Council, and courts and tribunals. More narrowly, 'the government' means executive bodies only: those concerned with the formulation of policy and the administration or execution of law. These executive bodies are the institutions to be examined in this chapter.

It ought first to be noted that the government in Hong Kong is not democratic: it is not elected by the people of the territory. The Chief Executive at the top is appointed by the Central People's Government (CPG). Tung Chee-hwa, the first Chief Executive, was chosen by a selection committee, required to be 'broadly representative' and consisting of 400 Hong Kong persons; his successors are to be chosen by another 'broadly representative' committee, this time of 800 persons. The Basic Law states that the method of selection shall be specified in accordance with 'the principle of gradual and orderly progress' and the ultimate aim is selection 'by universal suffrage upon nomination by a broadly representative nominating committee in accordance with democratic procedures' (BL45). Nevertheless the post-Tung method can only be amended with the endorsement of a two-thirds majority of all members of the Legislative Council and the consent of the Chief Executive, and this may mean that reform towards universal suffrage will be slow; in any event, the requirement of nomination by committee restricts the ability of Hong Kong residents to stand for election to or selection for the job. High-ranking executive officers are not elected but nominated by the Chief Executive and appointed by the CPG (BL48). Thus Hong Kong citizens have voting rights only in respect of legislators, not administrators (formerly, and perhaps in due course again, with the limited exception of Urban Council, Regional Council, and District Board elections, these bodies exercising minor executive authority). The government in Hong Kong must act in obedience to law, including law made locally, and cannot necessarily control the lawmaking process, yet it is constitutionally responsible to the Chinese government, not to the people it governs. Government officials often claimed during the British period that they operated through consensus, and that, by taking advice and seeking opinions from a wide range of boards and committees representing a cross-section of the local community, there existed a system of 'democracy by consultation'. A similar claim would probably be made by the SAR authorities (BL65 maintains the previous system of advisory bodies). All governments, of course, ignore public opinion at their peril: yet those which pay heed to it are not democratic unless a quite unorthodox definition of democracy is adopted. The government in Hong Kong is restrained, not by fear of losing the next election, but by its own notions of how it should carry out its functions, by responsibility to the Central People's Government and to the Legislative Council (BL64), by the remote possibility of failing to carry its legislative programme through the legislature, and, ultimately, by the threat of civil unrest by Hong Kong residents. Whether the system in Hong Kong operates effectively and provides good government is a different question from whether it is democratic. Democracy is, of course, a matter of degree, depending on which bodies are elected, by how many electors, and by what method.

GUBERNATORIAL GOVERNMENT

The focus of all government power in Hong Kong is the Chief Executive. In many respects the Chief Executive has metaphorically stepped into the shoes of his pre-1997 equivalent, the Governor. The adjective from the noun 'governor' is 'gubernatorial', and 'gubernatorial government' was as good a shorthand expression as any to describe the Hong Kong system under the British, and it remains an appropriate one. It means that the dominant institution exercising executive authority in the territory is the Chief Executive, who controls everything and is accountable to the CPG for all government action.

The office of Chief Executive is created by the Basic Law. The person appointed to the office must be 'a Chinese citizen of not less than 40 years of age who is a permanent resident of the Region with no right of abode in any foreign country and has ordinarily resided in Hong Kong for a continuous period of not less than 20 years' (BL44); he must also be 'a person of integrity, dedicated to his or her duties' (BL47). The Basic Law does not mention the possibility of his dismissal, but the normal rule would be that the agency which appoints him (the CPG) may also dismiss him; thus his principal loyalty will be to the Chinese authorities, not to the people in Hong Kong whom he governs. His term of office is five years and he may not serve for more than two consecutive terms (BL46). His pre-1997 predecessor was called 'Governor and Commander-in-Chief', though the latter title did not mean he had operational command of regular army, navy, or air forces in the territory. The Chief Executive has no such additional title and no authority over locally stationed Chinese military forces, though his government 'may, when necessary, ask the Central People's Government for assistance from the garrison in the maintenance of public order and in disaster relief' (BL14).

The powers and functions of the Chief Executive are set out in Article 48 of the Basic Law:

- to lead the SAR government;
- to be responsible for the implementation of law;
- to sign bills and budgets passed by the Legislative Council and to promulgate laws;
- to decide on government policies and to issue executive orders;
- to nominate for appointment by the CPG various principal officials and to recommend their removal;
- to appoint or remove judges;
- to appoint or remove holders of public office;
- to implement directives issued by the CPG;
- to conduct external affairs;
- to approve the introduction of motions regarding revenues or expenditure to the Legislative Council;
- to decide whether government officials should testify before the Legislative Council or its committees;
- to pardon persons convicted of criminal offences or commute their penalties; and
- to handle petitions and complaints.

The Chief Executive need not sign all bills emanating from the Legislative Council: if he considers a bill to be incompatible with the overall interests of the Region he may return it within three months for reconsideration (BL49). But LegCo may pass the original bill again, and, if it does so by a two-thirds majority, the Chief Executive may sign it or dissolve the Council (BL50). But dissolution carries dangers for him: after elections the new Legislative Council may pass the bill again, and if it does so (again by a two-thirds majority) he must either sign it or resign (BL52). This is part of the 'checks and balances' design of the Basic Law, no doubt borrowed from the United States system. Bills signed and promulgated become law; laws must be reported to the Standing Committee of the NPC which, in certain circumstances, may 'return' them, and they shall thereupon immediately be invalidated (BL17). Acting through the Executive Council, the Chief Executive is empowered under numerous ordinances to make subsidiary legislation.

In addition to the powers and functions specified in BL48, the CE appoints, summons, consults with, and presides over the Executive Council (BL55-6). He may act in opposition to the advice he receives, just as he need not accept the views of the Public Service Commission when appointing civil servants (when appointing judges, however, it seems that he is required to accept the views of the Judicial Officers Recommendation Commission (BL88)).

The executive authority of the CE comes from the Basic Law, but it is possible that the common law, through the doctrine of the prerogative, may supplement powers and functions expressly provided. This is a complex topic. The Provisional Legislative Council assumed, by referring to it in the Hong Kong Reunification Ordinance, that the prerogative, which before 1997 had supplied powers of government in Hong Kong, continued to exist in the territory. The CE apparently made the same assumption when he created an honours system (the Bauhinia awards to worthy citizens), a function which previously (pre-1997) belonged to the Queen in respect of Hong Kong. If the prerogative is indeed maintained, difficult questions relating to its content and distribution will arise. Nevertheless one might suggest that the task of the Chief Executive, like that of the Governor before him, is to govern and he may do all things required by that prescription which are not contrary to law, even if not expressly covered by BL48; and in doing so he can rely on common law (prerogative) powers.

Like the Governor before him, the CE may exercise only the authority granted specifically to him and the authority implied as necessary for the proper performance of his duties and conforming with constitutional practice. He may not interfere with the independence of the judiciary or of the Secretary for Justice in deciding whether to prosecute suspected offenders. Thus his powers are limited, and should he go beyond the limits, his actions carry no legal force: the courts may annul them. Further, he may be sued, both for private debts and for acts done in his official position, and he is not exempt from the criminal law. He must obey the law. By signing and promulgating bills he does, in a sense, *make* the law, but he must do so through the proper procedures and channels. What he cannot do is act as though the law does not apply to him. Should he transgress the law, it is the duty of the courts to treat him as in no better position than the lowliest citizen of Hong Kong. That, at least, was the position of the Governor, and it seems likely that the same principles apply to the CE.

THE EXECUTIVE COUNCIL

Like Cabinet in the United Kingdom, with which it may be compared, the Executive Council (ExCo) is 'the board of directors' for Hong Kong. It assists in the formulation of policy, though it has no independent administrative powers. Its role is primarily advisory: its function is to advise the Chief Executive. It is 'an organ for assisting the Chief Executive in policy-making' (BL54).

ExCo members are appointed (by the CE) 'from among the principal officials of the executive authorities, members of the Legislative Council and public figures', provided they are 'Chinese citizens who are permanent residents of the Region with no right of abode in any foreign country' (BL55). In colonial days it was usual for there to be more 'unofficial' (non-government) than official members, and Governor Chris Patten did not appoint members of LegCo to ExCo on the ground that it ought to be a 'non-party political body' giving impartial advice. It cannot yet be known whether the present CE takes the same view (it could be argued that he is *required* by BL55 to appoint members from each of the three categories mentioned there). Three of his ExCo members have been given responsibility for advising on distinct areas of policy, almost as though they are in effect, though informally, ministers on the British model of government. It is still too early to say whether this concept will be pursued in future. The Chief Secretary for Administration, the Financial Secretary, and the Secretary for Justice belong to Tung's first cabinet (the government's web page inappropriately refers to them as *ex officio* members), along with eleven 'non-officials', one of whom is termed the convenor. Four of the fourteen members are women.

The CE must consult ExCo, except in relation to the appointment and discipline of officials and the adoption of measures in emergencies, before 'making important policy decisions, introducing bills to the Legislative Council, making subordinate legislation, or dissolving the Legislative Council' (BL56). The advice he receives need not be accepted, but should he reject advice he must 'put the specific reasons on record' (BL56). It will likely be rare for the CE to decline to accept ExCo advice.

Apart from advising generally on matters of policy, the Executive Council has a number of other tasks. It considers administrative appeals, petitions, draft bills, subordinate legislation, and other matters. Meetings are normally held just once a week, and thus the Council is often merely ratifying decisions taken elsewhere.

The CE can probably ill-afford not to defer to ExCo, which is at the top of the consultative machinery of government. Though not elected, it is a channel by which the views of people outside the government can receive consideration at the highest level.

THE PUBLIC SERVICE

The Chief Executive and the Executive Council are, of course, dependent upon the civil service for the proper implementation of their decisions. Headed by the Chief Secretary for Administration and co-ordinated by the Government Secretariat, civil servants are organized into a large number of different departments, bureaux, divisions, and commissions; the most senior officials are the Secretaries and heads of departments. Appointments and promotions above a certain level are referred to the Public Service Commission, which advises the CE and whose advice is normally accepted. In addition to orthodox government departments etc, there are various councils, corporations, and boards which are public bodies exercising government functions.

All civil servants must obey the CE, faithfully carrying out his policies and enforcing the law. In accordance with the separation of powers doctrine, as executive officers they ought not to stand for election to LegCo, and, if appointed as judicial officers, they must sever their connection with the executive government. They are enabled by law to carry out only those functions granted to them and, it seems, to do that which a private citizen could legally do. They may be required by the courts, if necessary, to perform their duties, and a general duty to act fairly in their dealings with the public is imposed on them both by the needs of good government and by the common law.

THE LEGISLATIVE COUNCIL

The composition and legislative authority of LegCo are discussed elsewhere in this book (see Chapters 6 and 11). The Council is, of course, primarily responsible for enacting law, but it also has a role in controlling the executive branch of government. Members do not seek to act like an official Opposition in a parliamentary democracy (there is no possibility of forming an alternative government), yet they can and do raise questions about government policy and its implementation, criticize (occasionally vehemently), and propose alternative courses of action. They may do so during general debates, which are held on the Chief Executive's annual speech to LegCo and on the budget in March of each year, and through question time and adjournment debates (the government is required by BL64 to implement laws passed by LegCo, to present regular policy addresses to it, to answer questions raised by its members, and to obtain its approval for taxation and public expenditure). LegCo proceedings are broadcast and are open to the public and press, and thus the attitudes and opinions of members can be given wide publicity. The government is usually anxious to be seen to be responsive to views expressed in LegCo. The legislative chamber can therefore be important in influencing government behaviour, though this may depend on how representative of the general public it is.

Of greater importance in this respect is the Finance Committee, consisting of all members of LegCo other than the President. The Finance Committee considers the estimates presented with the annual Appropriation Bill (implementing the budget) and all proposals for additional expenditure. In practice, it can veto demands by government departments for more money, and its influence extends throughout government. Although it can only reduce, not increase, financial provision, and it cannot enforce changes to the taxation system, even in these areas it can make its views known. In this way the members of LegCo — all of them 'unofficials' —

can have enormous impact on the way the inhabitants of Hong Kong are governed. The Finance Committee's work is supplemented by the Public Accounts Committee, also consisting of LegCo members, which considers reports by the Commissioner of Audit. This committee is concerned to prevent waste in government expenditure.

In 1992 it was proposed to establish a Government–LegCo Committee in order to improve the effective working relationship between the administration and legislators. This never eventuated, and there is no such body in the SAR. The Legislative Council Commission, created in 1994, supervises the operation of the Secretariat and is responsible for providing administrative support, services, and office accommodation to the Council and producing official reports of proceedings. The Legislative Council Ordinance, enacted by the Provisional Legislative Council in 1997, establishes constituencies and provides for the election committee, the registration of electors, the conduct of elections, and such matters.

MUNICIPAL AND RURAL GOVERNMENT

In urban areas the Urban Council (UrbCo) exercises a variety of municipal functions, such as refuse disposal, pest control, the licensing of hawkers and food premises and funeral parlours, and the management of swimming-pools and playgrounds. It also provides such cultural services as libraries and museums, sponsorship of music and theatre, and management of City Hall. In 1993 UrbCo consisted of fifteen elected members, fifteen members appointed by the Governor, and ten 'representative' members elected from District Boards. But reforms in 1995, according to which UrbCo consisted of thirty-two elected members and one representative from each District Board in the UrbCo area, were objected to by mainland China; the Provisional Legislative Council thereupon created the Provisional Urban Council, to consist of not more than fifty members appointed by the Chief Executive. In due course, no doubt, elections of at least some members will be re-instituted.

Three aspects of UrbCo operations are of particular significance to the political and legal system of Hong Kong. Firstly, the Council is granted authority by the legislature to make by-laws and regulations on such matters as sanitation, markets, hawkers, abbatoirs, and disposal of the dead. Secondly, councillors are allocated to wards throughout the urban area; they work in ward offices hearing complaints and giving advice, and thus operate to investigate and settle local grievances. Some councillors are also members of the urban District Boards. Thirdly, there is an annual debate during which councillors raise issues not necessarily within the UrbCo sphere of affairs, and this serves as an additional, and often particularly well-informed, channel of communication between people and government.

The Regional Council (RegCo), established in 1986, has the same functions and powers as UrbCo, but in rural districts. It consisted in 1993 of twelve elected members, nine representative members (one elected from each District Board in the RegCo area), twelve appointed members, and the Chairperson and two Vice-Chairpersons of the Heung Yee Kuk. Like UrbCo its membership was reformed under Governor Patten, but again the Provisional Legislative Council replaced the electoral principle with appointments by the Chief Executive. RegCo has not adopted a ward system like UrbCo and has not yet developed an equivalent role in the political life of the territory.

UrbCo and RegCo are executive bodies with wide-ranging functions. Two other institutions deserving of discussion in this section are essentially advisory. The Heung Yee Kuk, established in 1926 to advise government officers in the New Territories, was reorganized under an ordinance in 1959 and now consists of a Chairperson and two Vice-Chairpersons, a Full Council, and an Executive Committee. The Full Council is composed of New Territories Justices of the Peace, the Chairperson and Vice-Chairperson of each of the twenty-seven Rural Committees, Co-opted Councillors, and Special Councillors, some of whom are elected by village representatives who in turn are chosen by the heads of households in 509 New Territories villages. The Kuk's objects, according to its ordinance, are to promote and develop mutual co-operation and understanding among the people of the New Territories and between the people of the New Territories and government, to advise the government on social and economic developments in the New Territories, and to encourage the observance of local customs. The Kuk primarily represents indigenous villagers. It has been a very successful pressure group in relation to New Territories land policy, basing its arguments on a clause in the New Territories treaty of 1898, and even in the Joint Declaration and the Basic Law the interests of landholders 'descended through the male line from a person who was in 1898 a resident of an established village in Hong Kong' have been protected. But with population changes in the New Territories and the establishment of District Boards throughout the territory it may be that the Heung Yee Kuk's influence has otherwise waned.

District Boards advise government on matters affecting the well-being of people in their districts, the provision and use of public facilities and services, the adequacy and priorities of government programmes, and the use of public funds allocated to the districts. Where such funds are made available, the boards can undertake minor environmental improvements and the promotion of recreational and cultural activities within their areas. They are not to be 'organs of political power' (BL97). Each board was formerly composed of elected and appointed members, with elected members usually in the majority; urban councillors and chairpersons of Rural Committees are also members of the boards in the 10 urban and nine New Territories districts respectively. Since 1982, when they were established, the District Boards have provided a useful form of popular participation in narrowly local affairs. In 1992, the Governor proposed giving them greater authority and discontinuing appointed membership, but his reforms were thwarted by the Provisional Legislative Council. Each board now (April 1998) consists of not more than forty members appointed by the Chief Executive.

In the second edition of this book it was stated that 'Hong Kong remains undemocratic, but the boards, the Kuk, the municipal and rural councils, and LegCo do provide electoral means by which government is informed about public opinion'. That is not now correct. In due course, however, with an elected legislature (though, initially, with only one third of its members chosen by direct election) and the re-introduction of elected members into the boards and the councils, Hong Kong will venture a little further — not far — down the democratic road.

LAW-ENFORCEMENT AGENCIES

A major function of the legal system is to achieve law and order through the criminal law, and the executive government seeks to achieve this through agencies devoted to preserving public peace and discouraging unlawful behaviour. The Hong Kong Police Force plays the foremost role here, with a large list of duties such as preventing and detecting crimes, controlling traffic, escorting and guarding prisoners, and preventing injury to life and property. The police are given wide powers of arrest, detention, entry, search, and so on which ordinary citizens do not have. They are not beyond the law, however: if they abuse or exceed their powers they will be personally liable before the courts. The Independent Commission Against Corruption (ICAC) has the more limited function of investigating complaints of corrupt practices, but the Commission is also expected to devise means of preventing corruption and educating the public against corrupt behaviour. Officers of the ICAC are also, like the police, strictly subject to the law. Unlawful conduct by the law-enforcement agencies is, however, more difficult to investigate, prosecute, and prove. Allegations of police misconduct are considered by the in-house Complaints Against the Police Office (CAPO), which hardly ever finds them substantiated.

5. Imported Law

COMMON LAW AND EQUITY

In what sense can it be said that law is, or has been, imported into Hong Kong? Before looking at this question we must attempt to clarify two basic terms: common law and equity.

The *common law* has earlier been described as decisional law. The expression 'common law' has an inherent ambiguity, however, and in fact its meaning always depends upon the sense in which it is used. It may refer to law which is not local law: that is, the common law of England is law which is common to the whole of England and not confined to a particular locality. It may, again, refer to a style of legal system, such as the common law systems of England, Australia, the United States, Singapore, Malaysia, and so on, in contrast to the codified or other systems which exist elsewhere. Thirdly, it may refer to case-law, not to be confused with enacted law (legislation). Finally, it may refer to one particular type of decisional law, to distinguish it from another type called *equity*.

This last meaning of common law can only be defined in terms of its origin. Common law rules were originally developed in England after the Norman Conquest by judges who moulded local laws into a cohesive body of legal precepts applying throughout the country. The judges who performed these tasks sat in regular courts, established by the King, which became known as the common law courts. But parallel to these courts there later appeared a court in which different methods of seeking justice were pursued. This was the Court of Chancery. The additional precepts which were applied in this alternative system make up equity, developed in the *equitable* jurisdiction of the Chancellors in the Court of Chancery. Equity is decisional, because it was formulated in regular courts by regular judicial personnel, and it is legal because its rules and decrees can be relied upon by litigants and it prevails over common law. Nonetheless, it is said not to be common law in the fourth sense mentioned above, even though it is common to all England, part of a common law system, and not enacted.

If all this seems exasperatingly vague, and somehow circular, it should be sufficient simply to recognize that common law and equity are two separate systems of case-law. They are distinguishable not only by their mode of origin, but also by their nature: common law rules apply in an 'all-or-nothing' fashion, whereas equity is discretionary. Equity developed to ameliorate the harshness of the common law, to provide flexibility where the common law was rigid, and to satisfy a desire for a different kind of justice. It is now applied in England in the same courts and by the same judges as is common law, and both systems of law, as we are about to see, were brought over to Hong Kong.

THE RECEPTION OF ENGLISH LAW

In order to know the sources of law in the Hong Kong SAR we must first turn to the Basic Law, which in Article 18 states that the laws in force shall be the Basic Law itself, laws enacted by the local legislature, certain national laws, and 'the laws previously in force in Hong Kong as provided for in Article 8 of this Law'. Article 8 reads: 'The laws previously in force in Hong Kong, that is, the common law, rules of equity, ordinances, subordinate legislation and customary law shall be maintained, except for any that contravene this Law, and subject to any amendment by the legislature of the Hong Kong Special Administrative Region.' ('Previously in force' means in force on 30 June 1997.)

Among these sources of law our concern in this chapter is with imported law — that is, common law and equity, imported from England when Hong Kong was a British colony. At one time, Hong Kong also imported British statutes, but these were not included in the list in BL8 and in any event there were few British statutes still applying in Hong Kong when China resumed the exercise of sovereignty in 1997. But the content of the common law and equity is still affected by legislation enacted by Parliament (the principal legislative body in the United Kingdom) and, perhaps regrettably, it is therefore necessary to become familiar with the history of the reception of English law in colonial times.

When Hong Kong was first taken over by the British in 1841 the island's inhabitants (fewer than 10,000) were peasants and fishermen who lived under the rule of Chinese law and custom. Even if the first British officials had bothered to look for it and utilize it, the Chinese legal system as it existed in Hong Kong was scarcely appropriate for the kind of place the territory was destined to become. In any event, the new rulers were intent on establishing a legal system which was familiar to them and which was assumed to be far superior to anything found in the Chinese empire.

One of the first things to be done, therefore, was to introduce English law into Hong Kong. At one stroke was thus imported a comprehensive collection of rules, principles, standards, and concepts — both enacted and decisional — appropriate for the trading post Britain had established. From 1846 to 1966, the formula by which English law was received into Hong Kong applied all the laws of England which existed on 5 April 1843, the day Hong Kong obtained a local legislature. There was a proviso, however: English law considered not suited to the circumstances of Hong Kong or of its inhabitants was excluded. The intended result was to provide a basic source of legal precepts which, though developed thousands of miles away in response to the notions and traditions of the English people, could be fashioned in accordance with local needs and conditions.

The provisions which first incorporated this formula — later recast as section 5 of the Supreme Court Ordinance 1873 — drew no distinction between varieties of English law, though in practice Acts of Parliament and common law were treated differently. In effect, the cut-off date of 5 April 1843 applied only in respect of statutes: all Acts contained in the English statute book on that day, provided they were general and not purely local in nature and were not unsuited to the circumstances of Hong Kong or of its inhabitants, were automatically in force in Hong Kong. Acts of Parliament passed after 5 April 1843 had no operation in the colony unless they necessarily applied by their own terms or were specifically imported by prerogative legislation or local ordinance. Common law, as revealed by the decisions of judges and published in law reports, was considered, however, to be basically unchanging, and judicial pronouncements subsequent to the cut-off date could be applied to Hong Kong because they merely declared what had always been the law. This was a rather artificial view of the nature of common law and has now generally, though not completely, been discarded (see Chapter 9), but it had the beneficial effect of avoiding application to Hong Kong of a collection of frozen common law precepts. Developments in the common law in response to contemporary conditions were thus given local effect, although they could be rejected or modified if colonial circumstances so demanded.

As time went on, it became increasingly difficult to determine which English Acts were extant in 1843 and to discover accurate texts. Hong Kong's own legislature had been busy since 1844 producing statute law made specifically for the colony, and a vast storehouse of English legislation became unnecessary. In 1966, therefore, a new formula for the application of English law to Hong Kong was provided. It split English law into two types (enactments, and common law and equity), dealt with each separately, and deleted the cut-off date.

ENGLISH COMMON LAW AND EQUITY

By section 3(1) of the Application of English Law Ordinance 1966, English common law and the rules of equity were in force in Hong Kong so far as they were applicable to the circumstances of Hong Kong or its inhabitants and subject to such modification as such circumstances required. Common law and equity could be amended by legislation, but their operation in the territory was only to be affected by statutes which themselves had effect in Hong Kong. What was the consequence of omitting all reference to 5 April 1843? It might be thought that, since under the previous formula modern English decisions on the common law were followed in Hong Kong, the cut-off date had anyway become obsolete and that its repeal was purely formal. But it was held in the case of *Gensburger* v. *Gensburger* that the effect was to bring the applicable common law up to date in the sense that it was the common law which existed in England on the day of decision that was to be in force. This meant that if a common law rule was affected by British legislation, it was the amended common law which applied, whether the amending Act of Parliament took effect in Hong Kong or not. The case concerned the old action of criminal conversation ('crim con'), by which a husband could recover damages from a corespondent with whom the wife had committed adultery. Under the former provision applying English law to Hong Kong, crim con would have existed here because, although it was abolished *in England* in 1857, the Act which abolished it was never in force in the colony (the Act was passed after the cut-off date and did not otherwise extend to Hong Kong). Under the 1966 formula, however, English common law at the time of decision in 1968 did not include crim con and thus the action was not part of Hong Kong law.

By this logic Hong Kong had lost control over its own (though imported) law, since an Act passed in England, though without reference to Hong Kong conditions or the wishes of the Hong Kong government and not itself directly in force in Hong Kong, would, if it impinged upon the common law, indirectly affect the law applying in the colony. The local legislature therefore amended the Application of English Law Ordinance in 1971 so as to emphasize that the common law and equity were to be applicable here, notwithstanding amendment of them as part of the law of England made at any time by legislation not in force in Hong Kong.

But the situation was still not entirely clear, for bizarre results could yet be envisaged. For example, consider the doctrine of waste, part of English land law: it is regulated in England by a thirteenth-century statute which at no time applied to Hong Kong under the Application of English Law Ordinance. Was it therefore the common law of waste as it existed in 1267 which was to be followed in Hong Kong? Another example: the English legislature saw fit to abolish the common law writ of partition in 1833, yet because the Act which abrogated it was not in force in Hong Kong it was held in 1970 that the writ could still be used here (or rather it could be used here for the first time, since the abolition Act of 1833 had been part of Hong Kong law under the pre-1966 formula). In another case it was suggested that the mid-eighteenth-century common law relating to disorderly houses, regulated by an Act not applicable to Hong Kong under the 1966 legislation, was still in force in the colony.

A similar argument was, however, defeated in *Oceania Manufacturing Co. v. Pang Kwong-hon*, which relied on a rule that the repeal of a statute does not revive anything which that statute had abolished. This was applied to the provisions for the reception of English law: repeal of the old formula contained in section 5 of the Supreme Court Ordinance 1873 by the 1966 ordinance could not revive common law rules which, by virtue of that formula applying the whole of English law as at 5 April 1843 to Hong Kong, had been abolished by Acts of Parliament which were no longer in force in the territory.

Where did this leave section 3 of the Application of English Law

Ordinance? The result was that the common law imported into Hong Kong *could* be affected by legislation made as part of the law of England which did not apply to Hong Kong, provided that such legislation was *formerly* in force here under the old formula. Therefore the cut-off date, despite having been omitted from the new formula, was indirectly still relevant: all statutes which were part of English law on 5 April 1843 and which abolished common law or equity continued to have that effect. Section 3 applied only to English legislation passed after 5 April 1843 or to earlier legislation which was never in force in Hong Kong.

This might seem irrelevant to the law of the SAR, because the Application of English Law Ordinance was declared by the Standing Committee of the NPC to be inconsistent with the Basic Law and thus is not part of SAR law. However, since the common law is identified as the law in force in Hong Kong on 30 June 1997, when the Application of English Law Ordinance remained operative, the extent of the common law must still be discovered by reference to the ordinance. This is why it is necessary to recall the history of reception and to understand the effect of the ordinance as affected by its predecessors.

Acts of Parliament which were in force in Hong Kong on 30 June 1997 and which lapsed on the coming into force of the Basic Law still have an effect on the common law to the extent to which, if any, they took away some aspect of it. It is the attenuated common law which was carried through into the SAR. The additions to the law which these Acts supplied of course fell away.

APPLICABILITY AND MODIFICATION OF COMMON LAW

The common law and the rules of equity were only in force in Hong Kong on 30 June 1997 to the extent of their *applicability* to the circumstances of Hong Kong or its inhabitants, and they could be modified to suit those circumstances. This rule was necessary if local judges were to be given an opportunity to mould the law into a set of precedents relevant to the needs of this place: the common law of England reflects ideas which do not necessarily prevail amongst Hong Kong people. During much of Hong Kong's colonial history, but especially during the early years, the unmodified precepts of a system utterly alien to the vast majority of Hong Kong residents would have made a poor instrument of social control.

It is obvious that the notion of what is applicable or suitable to local circumstances can vary widely from judge to judge, and the test can be either strict or liberal. The Hong Kong courts adopted a strict test: English common law was inapplicable to Hong Kong only if its application would cause *injustice or oppression*. An eminent English judge, on the other hand, insisted that a liberal and imaginatively construed test ought to be adopted. In fact there are examples of both approaches in colonial Hong Kong. Chinese customary law was held to govern various situations when English rules were considered unsuitable, mostly in the realms of family law and New Territories land law, and modifications ranging from the trivial to the drastic were occasionally made to applicable common law.

A few examples will suffice. The English law relating to succession upon intestacy (when the deceased did not make a valid will) was deemed inapplicable to the circumstances of Chinese inhabitants. English judicial decisions in the area of building contracts were at one time thought inappropriate in Hong Kong. For the purpose of the rule that a wife cannot give evidence against her husband in criminal proceedings, the word 'wife' was modified to include a concubine. A magistrate, when exercising the discretion whether to grant bail, was entitled to consider the greater likelihood in Hong Kong than in England that witnesses would be intimidated or bribed. The 'reasonable man' in Hong Kong is a different creature from the 'reasonable man' in England (the 'reasonable man', or better now the 'reasonable person', refers to a standard used widely in law, to determine, for example, whether a person has been negligent or provoked).

Although Hong Kong now receives the common law and equity of 30 June 1997, the applicability test and the need for modification will no doubt continue, and the common law and equity of some later date will be regarded as fundamentally the same (in accordance with the 'declaratory theory' (see Chapter 9)). A healthy legal system is responsive to the needs and aspirations of the community it serves, and it is an important task of judges in Hong Kong to ensure that imported rules of law are wisely adapted to suit local circumstances.

We are now in a position to summarize the reception of English common law (and equity). The enquirer must first turn to Article 8 of the Basic Law, from which it is learnt that any rule of common law alleged to be in force in the SAR must: (1) not be in contravention of the Basic Law; (2) have been in force in Hong Kong on 30 June 1997; and (3) have not been abrogated by the SAR legislature. In order to pass the test in (2) the rule must either on that day have been part of the common law of England and not inapplicable to Hong Kong, or, if not part of English law on that day (by virtue of abrogation by legislation in England which was not extended to Hong Kong), have been part of English law on 5 April 1843, not inapplicable to Hong Kong, and not abolished by legislation during the colonial period. This can be illustrated in Figure 5.1.

BRITISH LEGISLATION

Section 4 of the Application of English Law Ordinance provided for the reception in Hong Kong of prerogative legislation and Acts of the United Kingdom Parliament. Since such legislation is omitted from the specification in BL8 of the laws previously in force, it did not have a seat on the through train to the SAR. Acts of Parliament etc. cannot be in force in Hong Kong now — although, as we have seen, they have in the past had an impact on the common law by removing some portion of it and that effect still exists. But there is an exception: Acts and Orders in Council etc. which have previously been incorporated into Hong Kong law *by ordinance* are not affected. The Standing Committee of the NPC decided on 23 February 1997 that 'provisions [in ordinances and subordinate legislation previously in force] referring to any English law may continue to be applicable by reference as a transitional arrangement pending their amendment by the HKSAR, provided that they are not prejudicial to the sovereignty of the PRC and do not contravene the provisions of the Basic Law'. This would embrace such matters as the practice of the Supreme Court of Judicature in England and the practice and procedure of criminal cases in English courts. Not all the precepts which fall within such categories are considered to be precepts of law, but many of them are; even Acts of Parliament have occasionally been applied in Hong Kong under these provisions, though they did not come within section 4 of the Application of English Law Ordinance. There are a few other ordinances which contain a limited general application

Figure 5.1 How to Determine Whether a Decisional Rule is Part of HKSAR Law

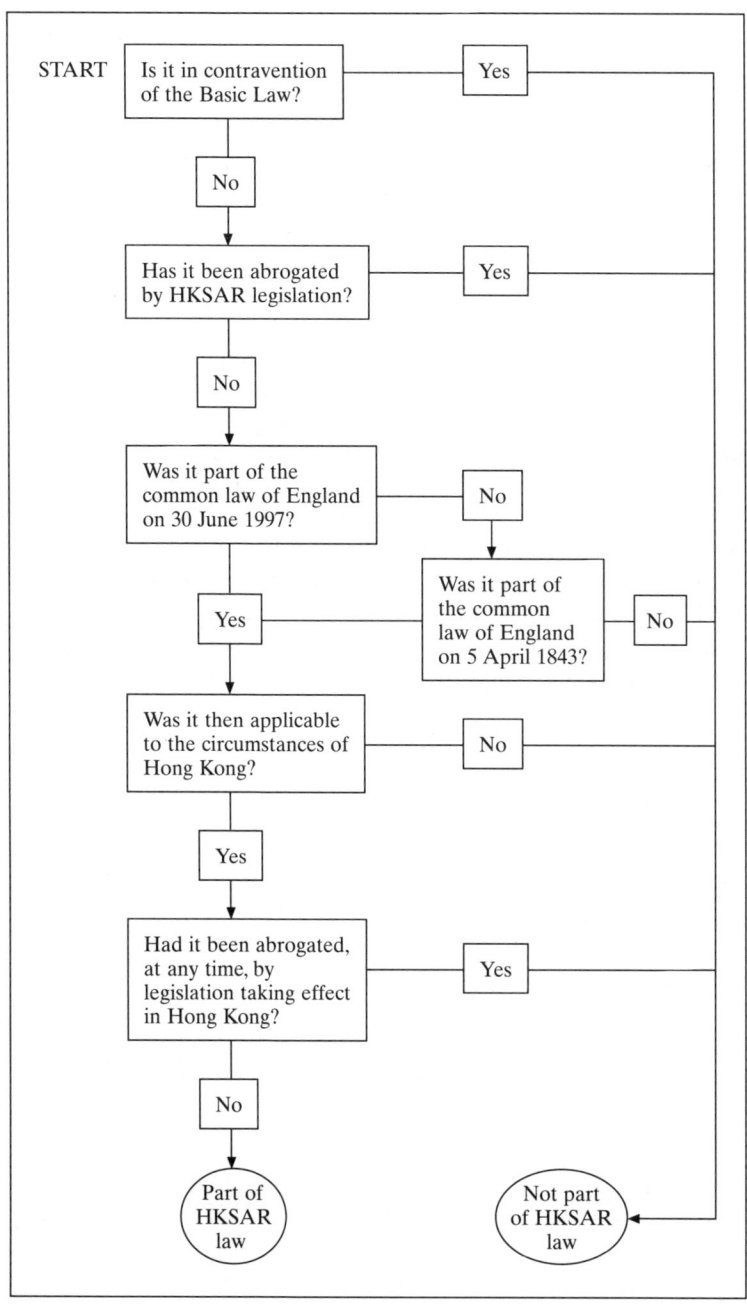

of English law, such as the Jury Ordinance: the law in force in England relating to juries shall in certain circumstances have force and effect within the territory. Some statutes empower Hong Kong judges to act in particular areas as would their English counterparts, and these can mean that English law, including Acts of Parliament, is received here. Such provisions will in due course be replaced, though to replace some of them will probably prove difficult. Until this happens, the imported law of the SAR includes some Acts of the Parliament of the former sovereign.

NATIONAL LAWS

Article 18 of the Basic Law states that 'National laws shall not be applied in the Hong Kong SAR except for those listed in Annex III to this Law. The laws listed therein shall be applied locally by way of promulgation or legislation by the Region'. The expression 'national laws' is not defined, but it presumably means decisions, resolutions, orders, declarations, regulations, and laws made by the NPC or its Standing Committee. There were six of these when the Basic Law came into effect, and a further five were added on 1 July 1997. As national laws they presumably prevail over ordinances. They are 'imported' from mainland China, just as Hong Kong as a British colony once imported Acts of Parliament.

6. Law Made in Hong Kong

PRIMARY LEGISLATION

The Legislative Council is declared in the Basic Law to be the legislature of the SAR (BL66) and it is authorized to 'enact, amend or repeal laws in accordance with the provisions of this Law and legal procedures' (BL73). This power to make law is exercised through legislative instruments known as *ordinances* which are enacted by means of a process to be discussed in Chapter 10. Proposed law (a *bill*) is introduced into the Legislative Council where it is read three times, discussed, perhaps amended, and, if agreed to, passed; it is then normally signed by the Chief Executive and brought into operation as part of the law of Hong Kong (BL48). The Legislative Council is a deliberative assembly; it cannot make law without the co-operation of the Chief Executive, who is not obliged to give his 'assent' (signature and promulgation) to a bill. The CE may, if he considers a bill to be incompatible with 'the overall interests of the Region', return it to the Legislative Council for their reconsideration (BL49). (The Governor could simply refuse to assent, though in practice he rarely did so.) The Legislative Council can then pass the original bill again, and if it does so by a two-thirds majority of all members the CE is required either to sign and promulgate it within one month or refuse again — and then, if consultations do not achieve consensus, he *may* (not *must*) dissolve the Council (BL50). This would indicate a crisis in government and it is unlikely ever to occur. After elections the new Legislative Council may pass the original bill again, and if it does so by a two-thirds majority, and if the CE's signature is once more refused, the CE must resign (BL52).

An ordinance is an example of formal, deliberate lawmaking. In the first edition of this book it was stated, then perfectly accurately, that the legislature could issue an ordinance on almost any topic with almost no restriction: legislators could convert into law virtually whatever precepts they wished to see enforced to guide the behaviour of Hong Kong people. But this is no longer true, because since 1 July 1997 the Basic Law limits the power of the legislature to interfere on certain matters, including fundamental rights laid down in Chapter 3. The Hong Kong Bill of Rights also, through BL39, in effect appears to restrict legislative authority (see below). The law legislators make applies to everyone and must be obeyed by all, including themselves, the executive government, and judges, provided always that it is not in conflict with the Basic Law. It prevails over the common law. But freedom to legislate is curtailed not only by topics over which it has no legislative competence.

In the first place, all laws enacted by the legislature must be reported to the Standing Committee of the NPC. This is 'for the record' and shall not affect the laws' entry into force (BL17). Nevertheless the Standing Committee may 'return' an ordinance if it considers it 'not in conformity with the provisions of this Law regarding affairs within the responsibility of the Central Authorities or regarding the relationship between the Central Authorities and the Region' (BL17). Any ordinance returned in this manner is immediately invalidated. (The same mechanism existed in the pre-1997 constitution, when the Queen could 'disallow' an ordinance, on any ground whatsoever; this power of disallowance was not exercised after 1913. There were also rules regarding the form of bills and limitations on the power of the Governor to assent to bills in certain categories, but these have no equivalent in the Basic Law.)

The authority to make law is very extensive. The courts may nevertheless declare an ordinance to be invalid (and thus void and of no legal significance) on the ground that it contravenes superior legislation. 'Superior legislation' certainly includes the Basic Law (BL11), and some provisions of the Chinese Constitution, and no doubt applicable national legislation as well. It does not include the Bill of Rights, unless (and this is not entirely clear) Article 39 of the Basic Law so provides. (Restrictions on the rights and freedoms enjoyed by Hong Kong residents shall not contravene the implementation of the International Covenant on Civil and Political Rights, and since the Bill of Rights is the implementation of the Covenant it has acquired a status superior to that of ordinances. This seems a sound argument, but it is not, apparently, one accepted by the Chinese authorities. The courts of the SAR have not yet had to consider it.) Inconsistency with superior legislation is perhaps the only strict limitation on the legislative competence of the Legislative Council: an ordinance may be contrary to morality, international law, or natural justice; it may be ill-considered or foolish; it may be retroactive (affecting prior events), unjust, or unenforceable — but it will still be valid, provided it does not contradict 'higher' laws.

Contravention of the Basic Law might be considered to arise, not solely in relation to express provisions, but where general principles of the constitution are discerned. Any ordinance which seemed to threaten the ultimate authority of the Chinese government over Hong Kong would be invalid. The doctrine of the separation of powers has been implemented in the Basic Law, and this may prevent the legislature from, for example, giving judicial power to the Chief Executive. Further, there is a common law principle which limits the territorial reach of any law of a 'dependent territory' and this principle could be adapted to apply also to the SAR. Accordingly, the legislature could enact ordinances only for Hong Kong — not for the Antarctic, or Brazil, or the Moon. This is said to be a restriction of competence to make 'extraterritorial' legislation. It does not mean that laws which purport to take effect outside the territorial limits of Hong Kong are necessarily invalid; it means that the legislature must 'mind its own business' and not interfere with someone else's. SAR ordinances which have some genuine connection with the territory would be valid (if not unconstitutional for some other reason), but ordinances with no such connection would be void and could be pronounced so by the courts. There is no mention of such a doctrine in the Basic Law and it seems unlikely that Hong Kong judges would resurrect it; in any event one may be confident that the legislature will 'mind its own business' when passing laws.

The restrictions on the power of the Legislative Council are much greater than existed under the pre-1997 system. There are many uncertainties, regarding, in particular, which provisions of the Basic Law set out principles or topics forbidden to the legislature and which provisions give guidance only. These uncertainties will be resolved by the courts, exercising their power of 'judicial review', and this reveals the important role of the courts in making the SAR constitution work.

SUBSIDIARY LEGISLATION

The primary legislature (the Legislative Council) cannot hope to enact all the statute law regarded as indispensable to a modern community. Therefore it delegates lawmaking authority, usually to members of the executive branch of government and often to the Chief Executive in his Executive Council. Delegates make rules, or regulations, or by-laws, these being referred to as 'subordinate' legislation (as in BL8) or 'delegated' legislation or 'subsidiary' legislation (as in the Interpretation and General Clauses Ordinance). In volume this type of legislation is very significant, filling out the provisions of ordinances by supplying detail. Rules, regulations, and by-laws must stay strictly within the area granted to them by their 'parent' ordinances; if a delegate lawmaker attempts to do something not authorized by the primary legislature, the offending subsidiary legislation can be struck down (deprived of legal effect) by the courts. This is an aspect of the *ultra vires* doctrine, meaning that the legislation is beyond the power of the delegate to enact.

COMMON LAW AND EQUITY

Hong Kong judges when applying the rules of common law and equity to the disputes which come before them have generally followed the example set by the courts in England. It was previously the case that, if a rule had been laid down by the House of Lords or the Judicial Committee of the Privy Council, it must be adopted by the Hong Kong courts. Decisions by other English courts were not binding, and local judges were free to prefer a rule enunciated by judges in Australia, say, or Singapore, or to develop their own alternative. This happened infrequently. Nevertheless, some English rules, even if declared by the House of Lords, could be considered inapplicable to the circumstances of Hong Kong or of its inhabitants, in which case some other law had to be selected; or an English rule required modification to suit local conditions, and the judges carried out that task. When this occurred, it could be said that Hong Kong's own common law evolved. It is probable that courts in the SAR will not consider themselves bound by any decisions in England, and although they will no doubt generally follow them they might strike out in new directions; if they were to do so, the small body of 'Hong Kong common law' would be enlarged. (See generally Chapter 9.)

CHINESE CUSTOMARY LAW

Under the pre-1997 regime it was established that, when English law was not regarded as suitable and there was no local legislation covering a particular matter, the law of Hong Kong prior to the general application of English law remained and was applied by the courts. That law was usually described as 'Chinese law and custom' and was assumed to consist of both the Chinese Imperial Codes and local customary law. The Basic Law, however, retains as part of the laws previously in force customary law only, not 'Chinese law and custom', thus giving rise to the possibility that the old Imperial Codes are excluded from operation in the SAR. 'Chinese custom or customary right' is specifically retained, by ordinance, in relation to land in the New Territories, which also seems to exclude imperial Chinese law. It is in the New Territories that Chinese customary law has its larger sphere of operation.

Several points can be made about Chinese customary law:

1. The customary law surviving in Hong Kong on 30 June 1997 (the date which determines the laws previously in force) almost exclusively affects family law generally and land in the New Territories. It was in such areas as marriage, divorce, adoption, and succession to property that English law was most clearly unsuitable for local (Chinese) inhabitants, amongst whom concubinage, ritual adoption, and the absence of a will-making capacity were taken for granted.
2. But very little family law according to traditional concepts now exists: it was abolished by various ordinances in 1971, and although rights and obligations existing under Chinese customary law in 1971 were largely preserved, in the course of time these will disappear as the people who now possess them die.
3. Customary law is both flexible and varied. It adapts to new circumstances, being capable both of losing force and of substitution by different customary rules. It is distinguished from English custom as a source of law because it need not have existed from time immemorial to qualify as law. And it can vary from place to place. There was never such a thing as the customary law of China: particular rules were usually restricted to a region, a province, a county, a district, a valley, or even a village, a clan, or a family group.
4. It is therefore unlikely that it could adequately be administered by a common law legal system such as was established in Hong Kong by the British. A judge, whether

Figure 6.1 Legal Sources of Hong Kong Law

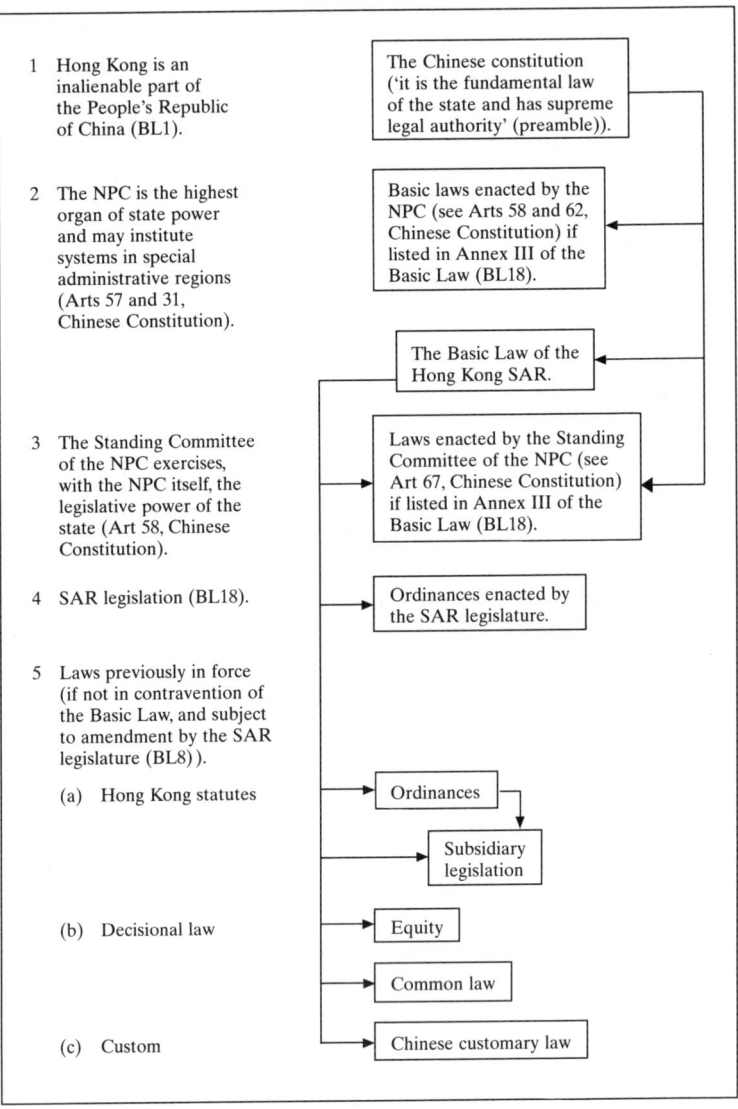

Note: The legal sources are set out in descending order of authority. The Chinese Constitution, possessing supreme legal authority in the state to which the SAR belongs, is placed at the top (it is unclear, however, which provisions apply to the SAR). Chinese customary law, which can be overridden by any form of legislation and is at the mercy of the judges who identify it, appears at the bottom. The Hong Kong legislature is established by the Basic Law and its ordinances are subordinate to it, though they are superior to decisional law and custom. Equity prevails over common law; both of these exist because the Basic Law specifies them as part of the laws previously in force and has established courts by which they can be administered.

English or, if Chinese, trained in English law, can hardly be expected to understand the intricacies of what are to him alien doctrines, and his habit of relying on and following precedent will conflict with the flexibility and localization of Chinese custom. British officials who maintained custom in the New Territories necessarily changed its character simply by the efficiency of their administration.

5. 'Chinese law and custom' could not survive if it was contrary to what English law looked upon as fundamental principles of morality; thus forms of slavery, or torture in the course of judicial proceedings, never became part of Hong Kong law.
6. Chinese customary law can, even now, be used to modify received English law or radically to affect the interpretation of a local statute; thus 'wife' in the Evidence Ordinance was in 1974 construed to include a concubine.
7. If it is correct that the Basic Law does not permit Qing statute law to survive, some decisions of Hong Kong courts which implemented that law in the former colony will need revision in the SAR.

From all these observations it is clear that Chinese customary law is, and should be, of little importance to modern Hong Kong. It is largely the law of a peasant community imbued with the culture of a bygone era. Obviously unsuited to urban life, it retains some relevance to parts of the New Territories, but is rapidly declining and cannot be faithfully administered by present-day officials. Chinese customary law remains part of Hong Kong law, however, and will continue to do so for years to come.

The various types of imported and home-made laws are displayed in Figure 6.1.

7. Literary Sources of Law

SOURCES

The expression 'sources of law' is ambiguous. It could refer to a *legal* source (the means by which law is created), a *formal* source (the theory which gives the character of law to an otherwise non-legal norm or precept), a *historical* or *material* source (influences contributing to the content and development of law), or a *literary* source (the means by which law is recorded and preserved). Hong Kong has three principal legal sources of law: legislation, decisional law, and Chinese customary law. Corresponding to the first two are the literary sources of the statute book and the law reports. Custom does not really have a literary source: it is recorded in the usages and traditions of human beings and is discovered by observation and evidence; it is not normally written down, though some lineage genealogies and other documents give expression to local rules. The historical sources of law are of course many and varied and cannot easily be ascertained and described. The formal source depends on the answer — perhaps *is* the answer — to the question: 'Why do we regard NPC decisions, ordinances, common law, and custom to be "law"?' That is a philosophical and political question belonging to the realm of jurisprudence, and we cannot even attempt to answer it here (see Chapter 1, however). This chapter is concerned with the statute book and law reporting, though, in addition, attention will be paid to published commentaries and other literary works on the law.

Legal literature can be classified as either primary or secondary. *Primary* literature is the law in its raw state: the printed ordinance or the published judgment (the judge's reasons for decision). Not all judgments represent actual law (some may later be found to be in error, or are abrogated by statute), nor does everything contained in them (see Chapter 9). *Secondary* literature is digested law: an author's analysis, discussion, explanation, and representation of the law in a particular area, available in an academic article or monograph, a textbook, or an encyclopedia. The article or book is not the law but the author's version of the law, dependent upon the actual law of the primary literature, but not itself the law and therefore inherently unreliable. Secondary literature is indispensable to the study of law and, by creating order out of what sometimes appears to be chaos, can be crucial to our understanding both of what the law is and of what it ought to be. In this way it can be a historical source of law, but it is not a literary source.

Actual law and commentaries on it can be, and are, recorded on computers; for present purposes a data bank may be considered literature.

THE STATUTE BOOK

All Acts of Parliament, ordinances, and delegated legislation are, of course, published: secret law is almost a self-contradiction, for how can law govern our behaviour when we have no means of finding out what it is? In Hong Kong there is a *statute book* — actually (at the moment) thirty-nine large, heavy folders — in which all current local legislation is placed. Known as the Laws of Hong Kong, this is a convenient and quite efficient source of statutory law.

Every Hong Kong ordinance is published first in the government *Gazette* (and normally does not come into operation until the day of such publication). It is given a number by which it may be cited: for example, the Revised Edition of the Laws Ordinance was No. 53 of 1965. In the earliest years, the *Gazette* was the only literary source of the colony's statute law, but in 1887 four volumes were separately printed containing all the laws then in force. These gradually became more and more out of date as new ordinances were added and old ones were amended or repealed. Further revisions appeared in 1904, 1913, 1924, 1938, and 1950. This series was replaced in 1966 by a loose-booklet edition which originally comprised the complete statute law of Hong Kong as of 31 December 1964. As lawmaking proceeded, the outmoded booklets were replaced and minor amendments were included by means of pasted-in printed slips or of handwritten annotations. The official who has responsibility for administering the statute book, under the Revised Edition of the Laws Ordinance, has quite wide-ranging authority to remodel ordinances by combining two or more, dividing them, renumbering sections, omitting spent provisions, and so on. If efficiently maintained, the volumes of the Laws of Hong Kong are fairly current (at least within the last six months) and complete.

Each ordinance (with two exceptions), along with its subsidiary legislation, if any, is assigned a chapter number and allocated to a folder in a position determined by its number. The printed page or booklet includes marginal summaries, annotations indicating the original ordinance and any amending ordinances — which can be separately consulted in the *Gazette* — and the source elsewhere, repeal, replacement, or amendment, if any, of various sections and sub-sections. If an ordinance is more than a few sections long, it is preceded by an *arrangement of sections* which provides a guide to the contents. A table of contents for the whole collection and a rather inadequate index assist in locating particular statutes. In Volume I a chronological table of ordinances is printed which enables the user to discover at a glance, firstly, the number and title of each ordinance passed in Hong Kong since the first one in 1844, and secondly, what subsequently happened to each statute, that is, whether it was disallowed, repealed, spent, replaced, discontinued beyond 30 June 1997, or survived to be incorporated into the current statute book.

The typical format of an ordinance can be illustrated by Figure 7.1, which is the first page of the Revised Edition of the Laws Ordinance (only the English version is presented). The running head (A) gives the page in the loose-leaf edition and the short title of the ordinance. Then comes, in bold type, the short title again (B), the long title (C) which contains a summary of the legislation's purpose, and the date (D), in square brackets, on which the ordinance received the Governor's assent (this was during the now-defunct colonial regime). Then the main body of the statute appears, divided into numbered sections, subsections, and paragraphs. Each section bears a heading (the loose-booklet edition uses marginal notes instead). Section 1 specifies the short title; section 2 defines particular terms — and so on for another nineteen sections. The legend at the bottom (E) informs us which issue of this particular ordinance we are consulting, which is in effect how up to date it is. Sections which have been amended since passage of an ordinance are followed by italicized words in brackets referring to the source of the amendments; for example, after section 18 of the Interpretation and General Clauses Ordinance appears '(*Added 89 of 1993 s. 37*) (*Amended 72 of 1971 s. 3; 3 of 1981 s. 2*)'. If a section is identical to or much the same as a provision in a United Kingdom or Commonwealth statute from which it was derived, the annotation sometimes refers to that Act (as for section

Figure 7.1 An Ordinance

A   2   *Revised Edition of the Laws*

B   **REVISED EDITION OF THE LAWS**
                            ORDINANCE 1965

C D   *To make provision for the preparation, publication and periodical revision of a revised edition of the laws of the Colony.*

                                             [24 December 1965]

1. Short title

This Ordinance may be cited as the Revised Edition of the Laws Ordinance 1965.

2. Interpretation

In this Ordinance, unless the context otherwise requires—

'commissioner' (專員) means the person appointed under section 3;

'effective date' (有效日期) means the date specified by the Governor under subsection (1) of section 11 for the coming into operation of the revised edition;

'Ordinance' (條例) means—

     (*a*)   any Ordinance enacted by the Governor with the advice and consent of the Legislative Council and any subsidiary legislation made under or by virtue thereof; and

     (*b*)   any Proclamation of the British Military Administration and any subsidiary legislation made under or by virtue thereof;

'revised edition' (編正版) means the revised edition of the laws of Hong Kong prepared under the authority of section 3;

'subsidiary legislation' (附屬法例) means any proclamation, rule, regulation, order, resolution, notice, rule of court, by-law or other instrument made under or by virtue of any Ordinance or Proclamation, as the case may be, and having legislative effect.

E   **Issue 13**   Authorized Loose-leaf Edition, Printed and Published by the Government Printer, Hong Kong

54A, Interpretation and General Clauses Ordinance, which is followed by '[*cf.* *1946 c. 31 s. 1*]'). The two pages in the loose-leaf edition which precede Figure 7.1 are a pink 'Check List and Instructions', which also give the enactment history of the ordinance (when and how it was amended), and a contents page.

The Revised Edition of the Laws Ordinance is somewhat special because it is the authority under which the 1964 edition was originally prepared and is now regularly updated. It, and the Laws (Loose-Leaf Publication) Ordinance 1990, are the only ordinances which do not have chapter numbers: they are placed near the beginning of Volume 1 (after the foreword and the indexes), and the other ordinances appear after the chronological table. Chapter 1 (abbreviated to 'cap. 1') is the Interpretation and General Clauses Ordinance, an important measure because it contains general rules regarding the interpretation, commencement, publication, and so on of all of Hong Kong's statute law. It is succeeded by its own subsidiary legislation and then by cap. 2 (the Public Finance Ordinance) and cap. 3 (the Jury Ordinance). This completes Volume 1. Other volumes contain ordinances 4 (the High Court Ordinance, with its lengthy subsidiary legislation called the Rules of the High Court) to 494 (though the number is steadily increasing) and 1,001 to 1,163. Ordinances numbered more than 1,000 are of a private or charitable character or are otherwise of limited application. Volume 39 (in 1998; the number of volumes tends to increase as the years go by) contains Appendices (former constitutional documents and the Standing Orders of the Legislative Council).

The statute book is, in general, comprehensive, up to date, reliable, accessible, and efficient and convenient to use. Since 1989, the government has determined to produce all of Hong Kong's statute law in both English and Chinese, with new ordinances being separately drafted in each language. This immense programme has now reached fruition (at least for primary legislation), and the statute book has been redesigned to accommodate both English and Chinese texts on each page.

The loose-booklet revised edition now remains, in respect of ordinances, the 'sole and proper law' as it stood on the last day of 1989. In 1990, the Attorney General was authorized to produce, in addition to the loose-booklet volumes, a loose-leaf edition. The advantage of the new work is that new or replacement pages can be inserted and thus amendments are more tidily and reliably incorporated; the redesigned format makes it easier to include parallel texts in Chinese. The loose-leaf edition has now replaced the collection of booklets lawyers have used since 1966.

A further innovation is the installation of the statute book (in both languages) on a computerized database, allowing quick and easy access to any item, key-word searching, and all the other benefits and frustrations that modern information technology brings. This system is called BLIS and can be accessed, without cost, at <www.justice.gov.hk>.

LAW REPORTING

Decisional law tells us what law is from the manner in which disputes have been settled by the courts. Judges interpret statutes, which is sometimes a difficult and subtle process; they also find and formulate the rules of the common law and equity, and in applying them to new combinations of facts they refine them and mould them and illustrate their sphere of operation. Judicial decisions usually have some precedential value: the rules and principles of law they use to resolve disputes ought to be employed in the future to resolve similar disputes if the law is to be consistent and predictable and if citizens are to be accorded equal treatment. In many cases judges have no choice but to follow earlier decisions (see the doctrine of precedent in Chapter 9). It is therefore important that judges explain their reasoning processes, that these explanations be reduced to written form, and that we have access to the records of judgments in previous cases. That is why *law reporting* is regarded as essential to the common law system of justice.

A proper judgment typically consists of three parts: an analysis of the facts which have been found by the court, a discussion of the relevant law, and the actual decision in the case, reached (supposedly) by applying the law to the facts. From the judgment we can determine the rule or principle of law for which the case is authority. If that rule or principle is in some way novel, the judgment ought to be, and usually is, published so that it can guide citizens, legal advisers, and judges in relation to this area of law in the future. The books in which judgments are published are known as *law reports*.

In England, law reports go back hundreds of years. Since 1865, a semi-official body, the Incorporated Council of Law Reporting for England and Wales, has systematically covered all the major courts and judgments and produced reports which are, on the whole, reliable and convenient to use. Private publishers, who until 1865 were the sole source of reports, continue to issue a number of series which also generally maintain a high standard of reliability and efficiency. Most common law jurisdictions have their own printed books of reports which are potentially available throughout the common law world. All this amounts to a huge collection: scores of thick volumes are published each year, and learning how to make use of them is an essential part of a law student's training.

Hong Kong had no adequate law reports until 1905. Prior to that year, the English-language newspapers reported on some cases before the courts, and often a complete record of evidence, legal argument, and judgment was preserved in their pages. Lawyers used to cut them out and paste them into scrapbooks. But this was scarcely satisfactory; in any event, no such scrapbooks seem to have survived to the present day, and our knowledge of nineteenth-century decisional law in Hong Kong is therefore very slim. The establishment of the Hong Kong Law Reports in 1905 was an important event for the Hong Kong legal system. The series has been maintained ever since, with at least one volume published in each succeeding year of British government (interrupted, of course, by the Japanese occupation of 1941–5).

The Hong Kong Law Reports are currently produced by a part-time editor who is also a registrar in the Supreme Court, assisted by a deputy, an editorial board chaired by a justice of the Court of Appeal, and several 'reporters' (lawyers or law teachers). The editorial team take the typescript of a judgment, edit it where necessary (correcting obvious minor errors and perhaps excising passages of no relevance to the main issue; these changes are vetted by the appropriate judge), prepare a headnote (which is a summary of the facts and the decision) and index headings or 'catchwords', list the authorities cited by and to the court, and check the proofs. (See Figure 7.2.) The printed version is bound up with other judgments and included in a monthly publication which is despatched to subscribers and sold in the Government Publications Centre and some bookshops. At the end of the year, complete lists of cases reported and cases cited are issued along with a comprehensive index. Cumulative indexes are also published every few years. In this way all important judgments by the Supreme Court and the

Figure 7.2 A Law Report

A	Lai Foon-yung	Claimant (Applicant)
	and	
B	Tin Sum Valley Public Primary School	Defendant (Respondent)
C	(High Court)	
D	(Labour Tribunal Appeal No. 7 of 1985)	

E Hunter, J.
F **1st July 1985.**
G Employment — damages for wrongful dismissal — measure to be applied.

H This was an appeal from the decision of the Presiding Officer of the Labour Tribunal awarding damages of one month's salary on a claim for wrongful dismissal. In his decision the Presiding Officer had relied on s. 7(1) of the Employment Ordinance (*Cap.* 57). The Employment Agreement provided for employment for one school year, whereas the conditions of service provided for a probationary period of two years. There was provision for termination by the teacher by one month's notice during the probationary period and by three months' notice thereafter, whereas the provision for termination by the school first of all referred to unsatisfactory service and verbal and written warnings but concluded:—

'Where it is considered necessary to terminate a teacher's appointment for reasons other than unsatisfactory service, the foregoing periods of notice should apply.'

I **Held:**
  1. **The provision for a two-year probationary period in the conditions of service did not convert the contract for one year into a contract for two years.**
  2. **Following the Common Law principle, the claimant was limited to one month's salary by way of damages, that being the period of notice under her contract. Section 7(1) of the Employment Ordinance is a statutory reenactment of the Common Law principle.** (*Gunton v. the London Borough of Richmond-upon-Thames* **applied**.)

J Appeal dismissed.

K S. C. Siu instructed by W. I. Cheung & Co. for the appellant.
   Louis Chan instructed by Tong, Kan & Ho for the respondent.

L **Cases cited in the judgment:—**
   1. Gunton v. The London Borough of Richmond-upon-Thames [1980] 3 All ER 577
   2. British Guiana Credit Corportion v. Da Silva [1965] 1 WLR 248

Note: A and B: the names of the parties; C: the court: D. the registry reference; E: the name of the judge; F: the date of the hearing; G: the 'catchwords' or index headings, enabling the reader to see at a glance what the case is about; H: a summary of the facts; I: a summary of the findings and the rule of law applied; J: the outcome of the proceedings; K: the lawyers (barristers and solicitors) involved; L: cases cited in the judgement. All this is the 'headnote', prepared by the Hong Kong Law Reports; it is followed by the actual judgment. The case is reported at [1986] H.K.L.R. 128.

District Court are made available to the public in a permanent and readily accessible form and within a fairly short time. Separate publications deal with decisions by the Inland Revenue Board of Review and the Lands Tribunal and with practice directions issuing from the High Court. Conveyancing and property cases were separately reported from 1980 to 1993. The Hong Kong Law Reports were in 1996 taken over by a private publishing company, with the Digest currently incorporated into it, and they are now known by the initials HKLRD. A new series of reports of public law cases made its appearance in 1991. Three years later a commercial firm produced Hong Kong Cases, an alternative set of reports which is a little more comprehensive than the Hong Kong Law Reports (supposedly the 'official' version) and which has absorbed the Hong Kong Public Law Reports.

In addition to these sources, every written judgment of the superior courts in Hong Kong is cyclostyled and lodged in the libraries of the Supreme Court and the Bar; the Faculty of Law at the University of Hong Kong has a fairly complete collection of them, and they are frequently used by law academics. Judgments dealing with personal injuries and sentences in criminal cases are also summarized and published in the *Hong Kong Law Journal*, and draft headnotes prepared by Hong Kong Law Reports personnel are circulated amongst the legal profession. Thus lawyers and judges can quite easily get hold of all judgments of comparatively recent times.

There are also various publications which assist in the locating of relevant primary sources. As one can imagine, the law reports of the common law are so numerous that they would be largely unusable without indexes and digests. In Hong Kong there is a series of books collectively known as *Addison's Digests* which consist of summaries of published and unpublished judgments systematically organized, indexed, and cross-referenced. Since 1985, a commercial publication issued monthly, called *Hong Kong Law Digest*, has provided a quick and complete guide to contemporary developments in the law, including ordinances, subsidiary legislation, judgments, and scholarly articles (now packaged with the Hong Kong Law Reports). Many unreported judgments are currently stored on computer and it is hoped that the judiciary will soon make these available to the general public. The *Basic Law and Human Rights Bulletin*, carrying digests of and notes and comments on cases under the Bill of Rights and the Basic Law, has been published from the Faculty of Law at the University of Hong Kong since 1992. Hong Kong Cases and the Hong Kong Law Reports and Digest, as well as materials from many other jurisdictions, are available on CD-ROM. Databases such as Lexis and Westlaw provide access to vast quantities of legal data from overseas. With all these aids it is possible, at least in theory, to be quite quickly and comprehensively informed about law directly or potentially affecting the territory. (For a more detailed account of legal sources of law in Hong Kong see Jill Cottrell, *Legal Research: A Guide for Hong Kong Students* (1997).)

SECONDARY MATERIALS

Until the 1960s, there were no full-time law academics in Hong Kong and consequently there was scarcely any secondary legal literature on Hong Kong law: it is part of an academic's duties to carry out research and to publish the results, whereas few practising lawyers have had the time or incentive to contribute to scholarship. Studies leading to a local law degree did not begin in Hong Kong until 1969 when the Department of Law at the University of Hong Kong was established. In 1971, the *Hong Kong Law Journal* commenced publication, containing the fruits of research, and this has been of considerable value to the legal system. Published in three parts per year, each annual volume contains scholarly articles and notes, commentaries on recent cases and other legal developments, book reviews, digests of personal injuries and sentencing judgments (though the latter have been recently discontinued), and editorial-style comments. The main focus of the journal's material is the law of Hong Kong. In 1992, a law journal edited at the City University made its first appearance.

Another source of secondary literature is the annual book of lectures on local topics delivered to practitioners. This has been regularly published since 1974. In addition, scholars occasionally contribute articles on Hong Kong matters to learned journals overseas, and quite recently there has been the welcome development of books written for a largely local market. This trend is likely to continue, and indeed has reached the proportions of a minor industry, to the lasting benefit — if quality is maintained — of the legal system. Some areas of law will probably always remain under-researched, but at least Hong Kong law is now being studied in its Hong Kong context and commented on by specialists who have some understanding of the territory's needs and aspirations. This contributes to the localization of the law.

8. The Courts

THE popular imagery of the law is probably centred upon the courts, in which the dramas of criminal prosecution and civil litigation are played out. Most legal disputes in fact never reach a courtroom — yet the court system is fundamental to the operation of the law and indispensable to its understanding. The Basic Law provides that the judicial system previously practised in Hong Kong shall be maintained except for changes consequent upon establishment of the Court of Final Appeal (BL81); that court shall be vested with the 'power of final adjudication' (BL82); the courts may refer to precedents of other common law jurisdictions (BL84); the principle of trial by jury previously practised, and in civil and criminal proceedings the principles previously applied and the rights previously enjoyed by parties to proceedings, in Hong Kong shall be maintained (BL86, 87); and the courts 'shall exercise judicial power independently, free from any interference' (BL85).

TERMINOLOGY

Several terms need to be defined at the outset. *Jurisdiction* is for the most part synonymous with power: a court has jurisdiction to do something when it has the requisite power or authority. A criminal jurisdiction is authority to apply the criminal law in judging the behaviour of an alleged offender; a matrimonial jurisdiction involves the law relating to marriage. There are as many jurisdictions in this sense as there are types of law, and each court is given one or more of them. A judge exceeds his jurisdiction, and thus acts wrongly, by deciding something he is not empowered to decide or by acting improperly in the course of the decision-making process.

Courts are either *superior* or *inferior*. These terms do not reflect the quality of the judges, or even the relative positions of courts in the system. A superior court has an unlimited jurisdiction within the territory; an inferior court's jurisdiction is limited by, for example, the value of the matter in dispute or the sentence of imprisonment which can be imposed. No court can, of course, exceed an unlimited jurisdiction, and thus only inferior courts are subject to supervision by other courts when they go wrong in this sense. In fact, however, the jurisdiction of every court is Hong Kong is restricted: many events occurring outside the territory cannot be brought before the Hong Kong courts, and in relation to particular matters judges are often constrained as to the order they are permitted to give in disposing of the case.

Jurisdiction is either *original* or *appellate*. It is the former when the dispute comes before a court for the first time. If the unsuccessful party or a person convicted of an offence 'at first instance' appeals to another court, that court exercises an appellate jurisdiction, deciding between parties now called *appellant* and *respondent*. In the original hearing the facts are established, whereas appellate proceedings are primarily concerned with whether the first court properly identified and applied the law. An *appeal* is different from judicial *review*, though it is not always easy to see how: on appeal all the law can be re-argued and a fresh decision on the merits given, but on review it is mostly the procedure adopted at first instance which is reconsidered and the original decision is either 'upheld' (confirmed) or 'quashed' (overturned, made null and void). Only the Court of First Instance has a general review jurisdiction.

In terms of substantive law, the main distinction is between *civil* jurisdiction and *criminal* jurisdiction. A court has the latter when it is empowered to decide whether an offence has been committed by an individual (the accused or the defendant) and to fix an appropriate punishment; the action is usually (not always) initiated, or *prosecuted*, by the government of the Region (meaning in practice the police or the Department of Justice). A civil jurisdiction is the authority to settle disputes between citizens, or between citizens and the government, when one party (the plaintiff) claims the other (the defendant) has acted wrongly and to the first party's detriment. The judge's duty is to decide whether the claim is established and, if it is, to determine the appropriate remedy (for example, the amount of monetary compensation). It must be admitted that such an explanation is not very satisfactory: a civil jurisdiction involves civil law, but we have no clear distinction between civil and criminal law (we just use different terms for the parties, the process, the outcome, and so on). Lawyers believe, however, that they know the difference, and the legal system functions effectively despite our inability to provide definitions which are not circular.

Another pair of terms needing clarification are *inquisitorial* and *adversarial* (or *accusatorial*). They relate to the manner or procedure in which a court or tribunal carries out its task. In the former, the official *inquisitor* is actively concerned in the case, making enquiries, asking questions, and involving himself in every aspect of the proceedings. This is more characteristic of systems found on the continent of Europe. Common law systems, as in Hong Kong, adopted the adversarial mode according to which the judge remains relatively aloof from a formalized mode of trial conducted by lawyers representing plaintiff (or prosecution) and defendant (or accused). The parties are adversaries fighting out their disagreement through legal argument in the courtroom. The judge is the impartial umpire or referee, his neutrality and dignity emphasized by the architecture of the court, the clothes he wears, and his refusal to 'enter the arena'. Some tribunals are less formal than, for example, the superior courts and tend towards the inquisitorial, though their primary obligation is to apply adversarial procedures.

Finally, some institutions for settling disputes are called *courts* and others are called *tribunals*, but the similarities are more marked than the differences: each type of first-instance body decides questions of fact and of law, and adjudicates between two or more parties. Some tribunals, though not all, are relatively informal, and may, for example, refuse to allow lawyers to appear before them, but there is no all-embracing definition which determines whether a body is a court rather than a tribunal. We rely on the dictate of the legislature for the term we use.

MAGISTRACIES

Most minor crime is dealt with by magistrates, whose primary jurisdiction is over *summary* offences (for which trial by jury is not available). Some *indictable* offences, however, which would otherwise be tried by judge and jury, may be disposed of summarily by a magistrate. Other indictable offences must be transferred following an application to that effect, or the magistrate conducts *committal proceedings* in respect of them: that is, a preliminary inquiry is held in the presence of the accused, and the magistrate determines whether there is sufficient evidence for a proper trial to be held. If the evidence is strong enough, the magistrate orders that the accused stand committed for trial in the Court of First Instance.

A magistrate may also issue various warrants, bind a person over to keep the peace, make orders for the payment of civil debts, award compensation (not exceeding $5,000), and grant bail. He or she can review his or her own decision, on application by either party, and may be required to *state a case* (an account of the facts, the grounds of the conviction, and the reasons why the proceeding is questioned) for the opinion of a judge of the Court of First Instance. The maximum sentence a magistrate may impose is two years in prison (three years in relation to two or more separate offences where the sentences are to run consecutively) and a fine of $10,000. Children and young persons come under the jurisdiction of a magistrate who constitutes a juvenile court.

Magistrates' courts dispose of a vast number of petty offences and are thus the judicial institution a citizen is most likely to have dealings with. They usually work under considerable pressure and frequently without the assistance of lawyers representing the accused, and appellate courts are constantly ready to override their decisions.

THE CORONER

A coroner, who is normally a magistrate, may inquire into the cause of or the circumstances connected with the death of a person. A jury (of three) may be empanelled. The coroner is an independent judicial officer whose functions are to resolve doubts about deaths in official custody or suspicious circumstances and to recommend how accidents can be avoided in the future. There are currently three coroners making up the Coroner's Court.

THE DISTRICT COURT

The long title of the District Court Ordinance 1953 begins: 'To establish a court, having limited civil and criminal jurisdiction, to be known as the District Court of Hong Kong.' The court stands between the magistracies and certain tribunals on one side, and the Court of First Instance on the other. Its civil jurisdiction is in general limited to actions in contract or tort where the debt, demand, or damage claimed is worth not more than $120,000, actions for the recovery of land where the rateable value does not exceed $100,000, and equitable jurisdiction (administration of deceaseds' estates, actions for breach of trust, maintenance of infants, and so on) where the value of the interest is not greater than $120,000. Its criminal jurisdiction covers charges relating to indictable offences which have been transferred from magistrates on application by the Secretary for Justice. A district judge sits alone, without a jury, and may not sentence a convicted offender to a term of imprisonment longer than seven years. Certain serious offences (for example, murder and genocide) may not be tried in the District Court.

THE COURT OF FIRST INSTANCE

Section 3(1) of the Supreme Court Ordinance 1975 says: 'There shall be a Supreme Court of Judicature consisting of the High Court of Justice and the Court of Appeal.' In 1998 the Supreme Court was renamed the High Court and the High Court became the Court of First Instance (CFI), but there were no changes to these courts' structure or jurisdiction. The High Court has unlimited civil and criminal jurisdiction and applies both common law and equity. The CFI has a mostly original jurisdiction (though it hears appeals from magistrates and some tribunals), the Court of Appeal an almost entirely appellate jurisdiction.

The civil cases which are heard by the CFI are:

1. those which, in England, would come before the English High Court of Justice — in this matter, therefore, and the next, jurisdiction is dependent upon English law;
2. those which would come before the Lord Chancellor and judges of the Supreme Court in England under the Mental Health Act 1983; and
3. those which are specified in any other law, either at first instance or on appeal.

'Any other law' means, in effect, local ordinances: it used to encompass British Acts of Parliament, but since 1 July 1997 such Acts cannot take direct effect in Hong Kong. The references in the High Court Ordinance to the jurisdiction of the English courts is politically anomalous but is being tolerated for the time being until a new formula can be devised. Apart from actions in contract and tort, and so on, the CFI hears applications for habeas corpus (an important means of testing the lawfulness of a person's detention) and for judicial review (whereby decisions of government officers and other bodies can be scrutinized and, if found to be improperly made, struck down or nullified). The court may make orders prohibiting a person's departure from Hong Kong, or pronouncing an infant a ward of court, or punishing for contempt (where, for example, judicial commands have been wilfully disobeyed or court proceedings have been improperly disrupted). The practice and procedure of the court are set out in the voluminous Rules of the High Court which are made by a committee under the authority of the High Court Ordinance.

The criminal jurisdiction of the CFI also follows that of its counterpart in England, and includes that conferred on it by any law. The CFI usually acts through a single judge, but in all criminal cases at first instance (unlike in the vast majority of civil cases) a jury also sits to determine questions of fact; that is, CFI trials are of indictable offences only and a judge may not act summarily to convict an accused person. All serious crimes are therefore dealt with by this court.

THE COURT OF APPEAL

Above the CFI stands the Court of Appeal. It usually operates in three three-judge divisions, each under a vice-president; the Chief Judge is President of the High Court, including the Court of Appeal. Appeals go to it from the CFI, the District Court, and various other tribunals and disciplinary bodies, and a judge may reserve for its consideration any question of law arising on the trial of any indictment. Questions of fact are decided elsewhere: the Court of Appeal is concerned only with technical arguments about the law, and for most practical purposes it is the final arbiter of what Hong Kong law is.

THE COURT OF FINAL APPEAL

Until 1 July 1997 appeals from the Court of Appeal went to the Judicial Committee of the Privy Council exercising in effect the authority of the Queen to dispense justice to her subjects. The Joint

Declaration signalled abolition of this aspect of Hong Kong's legal system and its replacement by a local Court of Final Appeal (CFA). Establishment of the new court was controversial, in particular the arrangements for its composition. Its jurisdiction is exercised by five judges sitting together, and the five judges in any particular case consist of the Chief Justice, three permanent judges, and one judge drawn from one of two panels, either a panel of former Hong Kong judges or a panel of overseas judges. The Joint Declaration and the Basic Law stated that the CFA 'may as required invite judges from other common law jurisdictions to sit' on it (BL82), and the decision to restrict the number of such judges to at most just one in each case was thought by many to be both contrary to the Basic Law and depriving the Hong Kong legal system of expert and undoubtedly independent judicial personnel. The court is at the apex of the court system and its decisions bind all Hong Kong courts, but appeals to it are restricted and have so far proved rare. Only about half a dozen cases from Hong Kong were disposed of by the Privy Council each year, and it is possible that the CFA will be similarly — and at great expense — underemployed.

The jurisdiction of the CFA is entirely appellate. In civil cases an appeal lies 'as of right' from any final judgment of the Court of Appeal when the value of the matter in dispute amounts to $1m or more, and at the discretion of the CFA or the Court of Appeal where 'the question involved in the appeal is one which, by reason of its great general or public importance, or otherwise, ought to be submitted to the Court for decision'. Leave to appeal is required. In criminal cases an appeal shall lie at the CFA's discretion from any final decision of the Court of Appeal or any final decision of the CFI from which no appeal lies to the Court of Appeal. Again, leave to appeal is required and shall not be granted unless 'a point of law of great and general importance is involved in the decision or it is shown that substantial and grave injustice has been done'.

THE SMALL CLAIMS TRIBUNAL

Monetary claims founded in contract, quasi-contract, or tort, where the amount claimed is not more than $15,000, are heard by an adjudicator in the Small Claims Tribunal. The tribunal's jurisdiction does not extend to certain actions such as defamation or the recovery of money lent. The hearing of proceedings is conducted in an informal manner, and no barrister or solicitor has a right of audience. The intention is that, where the monetary value of a claim is small, proceedings shall be speedy and uncomplicated. Justice done at this level is probably of a rough and ready sort — but cases can be transferred to the District Court or the CFI, and mistakes can be corrected on review or appeal.

THE LABOUR TRIBUNAL

Monetary claims arising under contracts of employment, and questions concerning various rights of employees, are the preserve of the Labour Tribunal, acting through a presiding officer. As in the Small Claims Tribunal, proceedings are quick, informal, and uncomplicated by the presence of lawyers: though it is otherwise if a case is transferred to the District Court or the CFI. It is often of vital importance to dismissed workers that their quarrels with employers be settled as soon as possible, which is why the more cumbersome, though more thorough, procedures of the regular courts are not applied to such cases. In 1993, however, the Chief Justice admitted that the operation of the Labour Tribunal had for some years caused concern, and he hoped that improvements would soon be implemented.

THE LANDS TRIBUNAL

Tribunals for small claims and labour disputes were set up to avoid the expense and delay of going to the ordinary courts; the Lands Tribunal was established to provide specialist expertise in respect of actions between landlords and tenants and of compensation claims under various ordinances relating to land. If road works, Mass Transit Railway extensions, the control of obstructions affecting the airport, and so on affect privately held land, or if the government resumes land for the building of a new town or other purposes, owners can seek compensation from the Lands Tribunal. This body does not act informally, and almost invariably barristers appear on behalf of the claimants.

OTHER TRIBUNALS

There are many other bodies which decide disputes. The Immigration Tribunal reviews removal orders affecting immigrants; the Housing Appeal Committee reviews the Housing Authority's termination of a lease; the Lifts and Escalators Appeal Board hears appeals from a refusal to permit a lift or escalator to be used; the Obscene Articles Tribunal may classify written, sound recording, and film materials and determine whether they are indecent or obscene; and so on. The civil service, the police, the professions, and many other groups operate disciplinary bodies with wide powers over a person's livelihood. The decisions of all such bodies may be either (sometimes both) appealed to the courts or judicially reviewed and, if necessary, struck down. In 1994 the Administrative Appeals Board was established, with a duty to consider appeals from various administrative decisions. Similarly the Municipal

Figure 8.1 Hong Kong Courts and Appeals

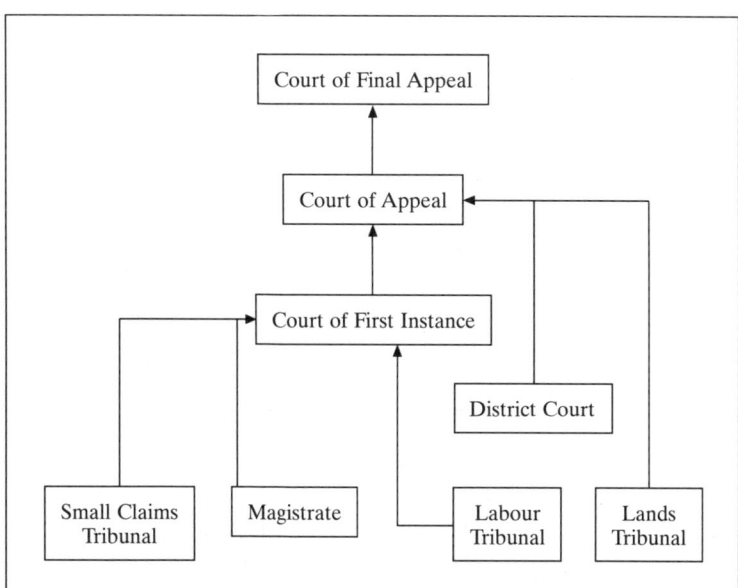

Note: This chart does not cover all of Hong Kong's tribunals, nor does it refer to connections between judicial bodies through transfer, review, or reference.

Figure 8.2 How to Determine Which Court or Tribunal Ought to Consider a Particular Matter

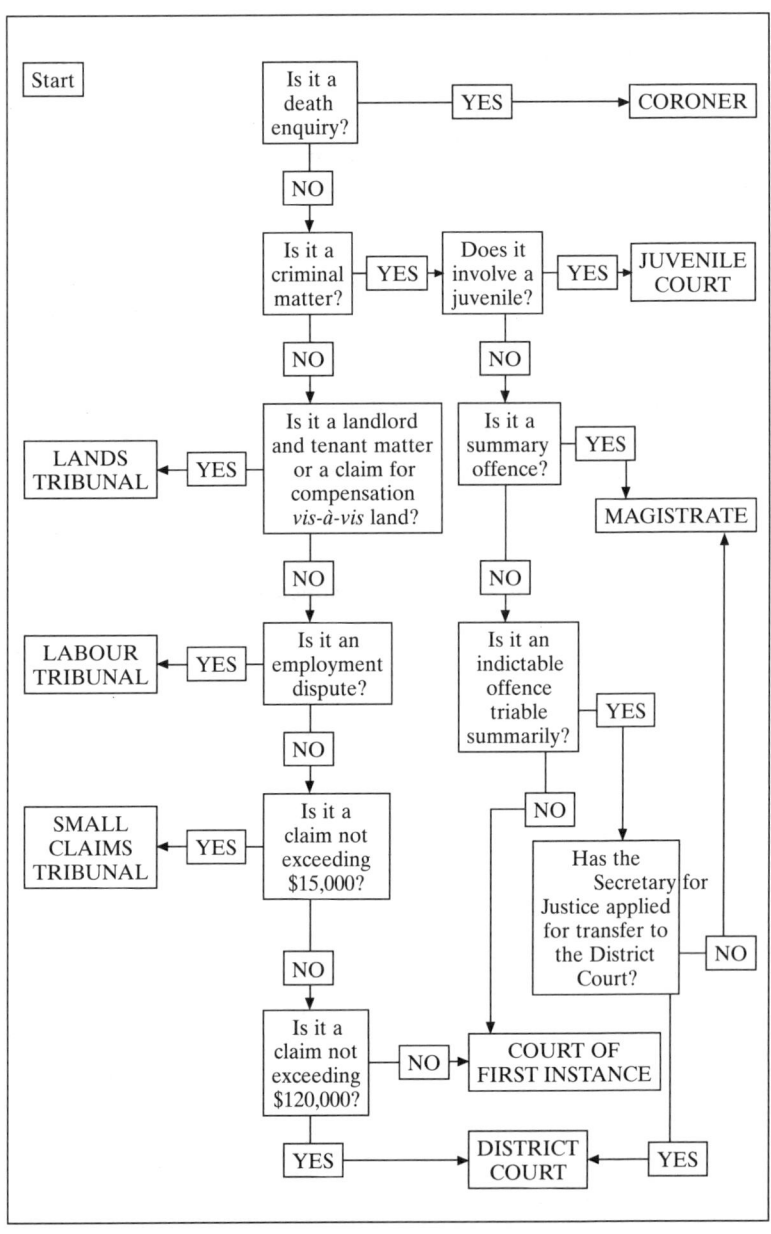

Note: This chart is for demonstration purposes only; there are a number of exceptions and complexities not included. For example, some remedies (injunction, prerogative orders) are omitted; much of the District Court's jurisdiction is concurrent with that of the High Court and this is not shown; some tribunals do not appear.

Services Appeals Board hears appeals against certain decisions of the Urban and Regional Councils. The Ombudsman considers and investigates complaints of maladministration.

APPEALS

No decision at first instance is ever absolutely final: it is always possible to have another judicial body reconsider the matter and determine whether justice was done at the original hearing. The Court of Appeal is, of course, the principal court for this purpose, adjudicating upon appeals from the District Court and the CFI in both civil and criminal cases, and from the Lands Tribunal. Magistracy appeals go to a judge of the CFI. From the Small Claims Tribunal and the Labour Tribunal a dissatisfied party may, with leave, appeal to the CFI and thence, again with leave, to the Court of Appeal. The District Court and the CFI have appellate jurisdiction *vis-à-vis* some tribunals and administrative officers, while most appeals from professional disciplinary tribunals go to the Court of Appeal. Sitting, like an underfed spider, at the top of this web of institutions is the Court of Final Appeal.

All the colony's courts and tribunals can be arranged in a hierarchy according to the lines of appeal and the weight (precedent value) of decisions, as Figure 8.1 shows. Compare this with Figure 8.2, which sets out in flow chart form the jurisdictions of the main courts and tribunals in Hong Kong.

9. The Operation of Decisional Law

DECLARING LAW OR MAKING IT?

Legislation is clearly and uncontroversially created by the legislature: we know which group of people made it, how they did so, what words and phrases it consists of, when it came into operation, and when, if ever, it ceased to exist. With most rules of the common law or decisional law, however, we know none of these things. We can cite a case as authority for a non-statutory rule, but the judge almost invariably justifies the decision by referring to previous cases which themselves were based on yet earlier decisions. There is no absolute, certain text of a common law norm and no simple, infallible test to determine whether it really is part of the law or not. We can rarely say with confidence when it began or when, if it has since been discarded, it lost its authority. Decisional law therefore seems so elusive that we may wonder whether it actually exists at all — yet lawyers and judges and writers constantly affirm that there is something we can meaningfully call the common law, that it can be known, and that it can be readily and regularly applied in the courts.

Even so, legal theory is divided on whether judges make, or create, or invent this law, or not. There are two main views. The first, and the older one, is known as the *declaratory theory*. This maintains that the common law is not made by judges but discovered by them and merely announced or declared; it is found in the customs of the people and thus consists of long-established principles which are law precisely because they are long-established. The act of discovery is often difficult, requiring training and skill and judgment, but it is a process of research rather than invention, of identification rather than creation. The law is always there: when concealed, it must be made manifest, not simply made. Thus law reports contain evidence of what the law is, though they are not conclusive. There is always a right answer to any legal inquiry, though it may not always be found. The judges declare the results of their researches, though their formulation of legal principles may need to be reconsidered later.

In modern times, this theory looks quaint and unlikely. There are many examples of decisional law applied today which could have no counterpart in an ancient era: consider, for instance, the rule that failure to wear a seat-belt can amount to contributory negligence. We can find no such rule before motor cars and seat-belts were invented; it must itself have been invented quite recently. But the declaratory theory meets this objection by drawing distinctions between principles and rules and between change and development. A specific rule is simply an illustration and detailed application of a broad, background principle. As more rules are enunciated the true principle emerges a little more clearly, but it does not change: rather, more of it is revealed by an incremental development.

The declaratory theory is attractive because it thus appears to explain the law's inconsistent virtues of stability and flexibility. Without adapting to changing social and economic circumstances the common law would have died out, completely replaced by statutory law. Yet it has survived, while at the same time seeming, at least in many areas, to be merely the modern version of traditional doctrine. The theory is also congenial to those who wish to deny the responsibility of judges for what they do: judges can be good or bad, successful or unsuccessful, accurate or inaccurate, but they cannot be accused of imposing their will on litigants, of creating rules of behaviour for citizens and applying them after the events which brought the parties to court — in short, of acting contrary to the rule of law. Nor can they be condemned for applying different law to different people in similar situations: judges endeavour to ascertain the true law and act upon it consistently, thus treating like cases alike. And to treat like cases alike is a fundamental obligation decreed by the common law notion of justice.

Despite its usefulness, is the declaratory theory a valid account of the judicial process? Many people think it is pure fiction, a fairy tale, and utterly misleading: development *means* change. Judges, when developing the law, change it, create it, *make* it; the common law is judge-*made* law and therefore identical to what the judges say it is. This, often called the *realist theory*, is the principal alternative to the declaratory theory and is now widely held. If true, it exposes the whole judicial enterprise to serious criticisms: judges are undemocratic, since they are not elected to make law, and unfair, since they apply new law retroactively. The first criticism is not very strong in Hong Kong, because government itself has never been democratic, though it will become stronger as the electoral principle becomes more firmly established here. The second criticism is at least ameliorated by the fact that judges develop the law infrequently; and when they do develop (or change) it, they generally do so cautiously, reluctantly, and at the edges of legal doctrine.

Nevertheless, most judges nowadays freely admit that in deciding what the law is they often have considerable room in which to manoeuvre. They can always choose which rules to apply, or what refinement of them is appropriate, or whether to make an exception to or an extension of an established rule. Their discretion, or freedom of choice, is most obvious in cases of 'first impression', where the particular point in issue has never arisen for decision before. Yet in most cases uncertain enough to require judicial settlement the judge can impose a personal view; indeed the role of a judge's subjective preferences is inescapable if judges are recognized as mere mortals, influenced by their temperament, upbringing, training, political, moral, and religious beliefs, and so on. The image sometimes conveyed by the declaratory theory of judges as almost machine-like, formalistic automatons, operating entirely impartially in finding and applying law, is simply unrealistic, and contrary to elementary notions of psychology. This need not mean that judges do not consciously attempt to do what the declaratory theory says they ought to do, which is to remain faithful to the law established in statutes, previous judicial decisions (if correct), and the social customs of the people. Some judges, however, are avowedly activist, creative in their desire to mould the law, to develop (or alter) it to keep pace with rapid social change, and to keep it in touch with modern ideas.

An analogy from quantum mechanics may help to explain how lawyers regard the two theories of adjudication. In physics there are differing pictures of, for example, the nature of light. Does light consist of particles or of waves? Scientists now generally believe it consists of *both*:

> [Both theories] are equally valid, complementary descriptions of the same reality. Neither description is complete in itself, but there are circumstances where it is more appropriate to use the particle concept, and circumstances where it is better to use the wave concept. A fundamental entity such as an electron is neither a particle nor a wave but under some circumstances it behaves as if it were a particle.... This idea of wave and particle being

two complementary facets of the electron's complex personality is called complementarity.

Similarly, the judicial function involves complementarity, in some circumstances being better described as the mere declaring of old law, in other circumstances clearly appearing as the fashioning of new law. This is known as the 'wavicle' theory of the common law. (It is my own invention.)

Judges, then, though bound by previous decisions, may, nevertheless, be simultaneously free, depending on how you look at it. This perhaps sounds contrary to common sense, and there is a more conventional explanation of the puzzle.

RATIO DECIDENDI AND *OBITER DICTUM*

Before exploring this question further we ought to clarify our terms. When a dispute comes to court the whole process of settlement is called the *decision*, which is an order in favour of plaintiff or defendant. (In a criminal case, if the accused has lost and is thus convicted, the decision of 'guilty' is followed by a sentence of, usually, a fine or imprisonment; in a civil case, if the plaintiff succeeds, the order will state the remedy, for example a sum of money as damages or an injunction.) The decision is announced in a *judgment*, which is a statement of the reasons for the decision. A judgment ought always to exist, whether oral or in writing, because the legal process is open and rational, and litigants are entitled to know why they have won or lost. A written judgment, or an oral judgment later reduced to writing, may be published in the law reports, and in any event may later be referred to by lawyers as evidence of legal reasoning or as containing a principle of law which must be followed in other cases. If there is just one judge, which is usual when a case is first heard, there will be just one judgment. On appeal, however, there may be three or more judges. If all are agreed, there may be a joint judgment — one statement of reasons to which all judges append their names — or a principal judgment by one judge with which the others concur. A judge who disagrees with the majority view delivers a dissenting judgment.

In any particular judgment there is a rule or principle of law which is applied to settle the dispute; the judge has selected an appropriate norm and used it to determine a result in relation to the issue before the court. The judgment is the authority for that legal proposition. It may not expressly formulate the proposition or state it in clear terms, but the rule or principle is, nevertheless, embraced by the judgment and relied upon. That legal precept is called the *ratio decidendi*. It is the reason for deciding; without it, the decision might have been different. It is a necessary step in the reasoning process.

It is the *ratio decidendi* which is capable of binding later judges. By contrast, other comments incorporated in a judgment — references to non-material facts, general observations on the state of the law, compliments to (or criticisms of) the lawyers who appeared, literary embellishment, and so on — are said 'by the way' and are termed *obiter dicta*. Most such *dicta* cannot, of course, in their very nature be binding. Legal commentary which is *obiter* may express a correct view of the law (a part of the law not directly and immediately raised in the case) and it may be highly persuasive, but judges in subsequent cases cannot be obliged to accept it as correct.

Legal theorists argue about how best to define the *ratio decidendi*, though all are agreed that the *ratio* exists or at least is a necessary concept if decisional law is to have any meaning. The following principles apply:

- Determining the *ratio* is not an automatic process; it is more of an art than a science, and reasonable persons learned in the law can disagree on the *ratio* of any particular judgment.
- Our perception of what the *ratio* is may depend on the treatment given to the judgment in subsequent cases.
- Therefore the judge's own version of the *ratio*, if explicitly stated, is not conclusive.
- The *ratio* depends on the relevant, or *material*, facts of the case.
- Each judgment has a *ratio*, and where there are two or more judgments in a case, the *ratio* of the case is determined by finding the proposition of law common to all the majority judgments, if there *is* such a proposition. It may be very complicated, and ultimately impossible, to discover one *ratio* from amongst several judgments.
- Much of the uncertainty in the process arises from the necessity to decide, firstly, which facts are to be

regarded as material, and secondly, how best to express the material facts.

To illustrate this last point, consider a famous example: a person drinks a bottle of ginger beer contaminated, through the carelessness (or negligence) of the manufacturer, by the remains of a snail and thereupon suffers mental and physical distress; the court holds that the manufacturer must pay damages to the consumer. In this abbreviated account a great many facts have been omitted because they do not seem relevant, such as the colour of the consumer's hair, the time of day when the ginger beer was drunk, and the sex of the consumer. These do not seem relevant. Why not? There is no simple explanation; it would certainly be odd to make liability for negligence depend on, for example, the colour of a person's hair. But what seems irrelevant to me might not seem so to someone else, so here is a possible source of reasonable disagreement.

The facts stated above do not indicate whether the bottle was made of clear glass or opaque glass: clear glass would have enabled the consumer to inspect the contents before drinking them, so failure to inspect might be regarded as fault on the part of the consumer, and the manufacturer might be thought less liable, or not liable at all, for the negligence. Thus some would insist that the opaqueness of the bottle was a material fact. Again, reasonable people can disagree on this.

To some degree I have generalized some of the facts of this case, or presented them in a more abstract way than is possible. I referred to a manufacturer, not to Mr Stevenson of Scotland; I mentioned a consumer, not Ms Donoghue. I was very specific in stating that it was a bottle of ginger beer contaminated by a snail — but I could have been even more specific and detailed by informing you that it was a bottle of ginger beer contaminated by a snail of one particular species. I could also have been less specific and more general (more abstract) by listing as facts that the consumer was harmed by a soft drink, or a beverage, or an item to be consumed, and that the drink was spoiled by a dead creature or a foreign body. How I perceive the material facts and how abstractly I express them will strongly influence the principle of law I draw from the case. My version of the *ratio decidendi* might be very narrow: when Mr Stevenson, a Scot, sells ginger beer in an opaque bottle to one Minchella, proprietor of a café at Paisley, who then sells it to a customer who pours it out for a friend, a woman called Ms Donoghue, and Ms Donoghue suffers from shock and gastro-enteritis as a result of a decomposed snail in the bottle, Mr Stevenson is liable to Ms Donoghue for his negligence. This is so narrow as to seem to me absurd: law should supply general standards of conduct, not detailed prescriptions for particular individuals. But how wide should the true principle of this case be? Should it refer to the liability of manufacturers of food stuffs, or of manufacturers of items to be used, or of persons who sell any commodity at all? Should it apply only to physical injury or to any kind of harm (such as financial loss)? There is no clear answer and no certain way of deciding: all depends on what seems to be appropriate, proper, and just.

Assistance can be gained from two obvious sources. The first is the majority judgments of the case itself. Two judges dissented from the decision and their judgments are therefore of no value in determining the *ratio decidendi*. Of the three majority judgments, the most influential contains in effect two versions of a *ratio*: a wide one and a narrow one. The wide version states that a person must take reasonable care to avoid acts or omissions which can be reasonably foreseen to be likely to injure his or her neighbours (a person's neighbours being people who are so closely and directly affected by his or her act that they ought reasonably to have been in his or her contemplation). Compare that with the much more restricted proposition that a manufacturer of products owes to a consumer a duty to take reasonable care when preparing products which, if carelessly prepared, might result in injury to the consumer's life or property and which are sold in such a form that there is no reasonable possibility of intermediate examination. Both versions, it will be noted, make liberal use of the word 'reasonable': but what is reasonable in different circumstances? Only a subsequent judge can say. And which version is to be followed in a later case? The original case offers very little guidance.

The second source of assistance, which is available to us now, but which was not available to a judge in the next case in which negligence was claimed in the courts to give rise to a duty to pay damages, is the attitude taken by judges since the initial judgments were written. There have been many attempts to limit the breadth of the principle by, for example, requiring the product to be for internal consumption, not external application (such as clothes contaminated by noxious chemicals), or the damage suffered to be to life and limb rather than property or financial interests. Most of these attempts have failed: the original case has been used as authority to found liability for negligence where financial loss arose from carelessly prepared information and from negligence by a solicitor, and where damage to property occurred when delinquents escaped from detention. In one case a farmer who lawfully sprayed his crops with pesticide, his act occurring entirely on his own land and not involving the manufacture or sale of a product, was held to be liable for negligence to nearby bee-keepers whose bees died after going on to the farmer's land and being poisoned by the pesticide. The judge consciously applied the wide principle stated above. Such cases are a long way from illness caused by a snail in a ginger beer bottle! They indicate that the broad version of the *ratio decidendi* has found favour with the courts.

The moral of all this is, of course, that a judge who is bound by the *ratio decidendi* of the 'snail-in-the-ginger-beer' case is not clearly directed, or enjoined, or ordered to decide that there was negligence in another case where the facts are somewhat different, even though it may seem that the same principle ought to apply in both cases. Just what is that principle? Are the facts of the second case *sufficiently similar* to make the principle applicable to it? The answers to such questions depend not on strict logic but on intuitions, or on feelings of appropriateness — and these can differ from observer to observer. Persons trained in the law often react in similar ways in such situations: their intuitions often agree. But they do not always agree, and one lawyer might plausibly argue that the facts of a new case are *distinguishable*, and thus the principle of the old one should not be regarded as relevant, while another lawyer assumes that the same principle naturally applies. The judge has to decide between views which might seem equally persuasive, and can only decide according to his or her own notions of what is correct. In these circumstances it is reasonable to describe the judge as making new law. At the same time, one could also portray the judge as finding the true extent of the principle to be extracted from the 'snail-in-the-ginger-beer' case. It all depends on how you look at it, because of the complementarity of the judicial function.

THE DOCTRINE OF PRECEDENT

Not every *ratio decidendi* of every majority judgment is binding in all subsequent cases. The doctrine of binding precedent or *stare decisis* ('standing by things decided') provides that, while all previous cases are entitled to be respectfully considered in relation to relevant subsequent cases, only certain of them contain principles of law which bind or oblige. This depends on the hierarchy of courts: a court is bound to follow a *ratio decidendi* emerging from a court above it in the hierarchy, and often a *ratio* of one of its own previous judgments, but may refuse to follow decisions of courts below it.

At the top of the hierarchy of Hong Kong courts is the Court of Final Appeal (see Chapter 8). The CFA will probably decide (it has not so far had to consider the question) that it is not bound by its own decisions, and on principle it is not bound by those of any other court sitting in Hong Kong. It is required to follow an interpretation of the Basic Law issued by the Standing Committee of the NPC (BL158), but the Standing Committee is probably the only institution, other than a legislature, to which it must defer.

Prior to 1 July 1997 the Hong Kong courts were bound by decisions of the Judicial Committee of the Privy Council (then the court of final appeal for Hong Kong) and, on questions of English law applicable in the territory, by decisions of the House of Lords. The latter body (a judicial institution, not to be confused with the House of Lords as the upper house of the United Kingdom Parliament) was not part of the hierarchy of our courts: its decisions could not therefore have been binding on the Hong Kong courts on the basis of any structural relationship. Local judges, however, traditionally regarded themselves as obliged to follow House of Lords' decisions in common law matters because the common law of England applies here and the House of Lords is the supreme tribunal for the identification of English law. Further, the judges who sat in the House of Lords also, for the most part, sat in the Judicial Committee of the Privy Council and were likely to decide the same way, so it would again be futile to disagree with the House when an appeal might go to the Council. In a case on appeal from Hong Kong in 1985 the Judicial Committee stated that it was itself bound by the House of Lords on a matter of English law, thus leaving no room for Hong Kong courts to disagree with the House of Lords. Even on matters of statutory interpretation (which are not common law and not English law), where Hong Kong and English legislation were very similar, decisions of the House of Lords concerning English provisions were in effect binding in Hong Kong in relation to Hong Kong provisions. The relevance of all this is that the CFA might consider itself bound to follow decisions by both the Privy Council and the House of Lords because they stated the 'law previously in force' (that is, the law as it was in Hong Kong on 30 June 1997), which is the category to which common law applying in the SAR belongs. In accordance with the declaratory theory, decisions of the Privy Council and the House of Lords after the cut-off date would continue to represent the common law as at 30 June 1997 (since the common law does not change), and thus the Hong Kong courts would be bound by those decisions. But there are ways of escaping this logic, and it would seem anomalous for SAR courts after the change of sovereignty to follow decisions by judicial institutions of the former 'mother country'. There would be attractive practical grounds for maintaining former attitudes, but these are unlikely to compel in the face of political independence.

The Court of Appeal in Hong Kong is obliged to follow every *ratio decidendi* in every prior CFA case. This follows from the fundamental principle of judicial hierarchy and 'vertical' *stare decisis* (being bound by decisions of courts superior in the hierarchy), but there is a practical reason as well: the CFA is likely to remain consistent in its view of the law from case to case, and when hearing an appeal it will tend to apply the law it has already stated. It would be a waste of time and money for the lower courts to differ, because a dissatisfied party would only appeal and have the decision overturned — with costs likely being awarded against the party which had succeeded in the Court of Appeal.

Hong Kong judges have never been formally bound by decisions of the English Court of Appeal or of other English courts. They have generally followed them, however, on various grounds: that it is desirable for the common law not to diverge amongst the various countries in which it operates (unless local circumstances are so different that English law is inapplicable or deserving of modification), that they provide a greater range of decisions than have been delivered in Hong Kong and thus give guidance to local lawyers, that to abide by them promotes consistency and certainty, and so on. Perhaps this habit of deference to English courts arose merely from the fact that Hong Kong practitioners and judges tended, through their training and background, to be familiar with these courts' decisions. Such reasons are likely to continue in the SAR period: even without a strict doctrine of *stare decisis*, the normal assumption will be that English courts best express the common law of England which applies in the territory and ought normally to be respected and followed. Nevertheless the Basic Law expressly states that the courts 'may refer to precedents of other common law jurisdictions' (BL84), which may encourage local lawyers and judges to rely less than previously on English decisions.

The rule of *vertical stare decisis* generally applies in the Hong Kong system. Thus all courts and tribunals must loyally follow the principles laid down by the High Court (Court of First Instance and Court of Appeal). The CFI obeys the Court of Appeal. The District Court obeys both. Magistrates, coroners, and tribunal officers ought to obey the District Court and the High Court.

'Horizontal' stare decisis (courts being bound by their own decisions) is accepted in Hong Kong at the Court of Appeal level and ought to be generally observed elsewhere. The Court of Appeal, in relation to itself, has however noted some exceptions: it need not follow itself where its decision cannot stand with a subsequent House of Lords or Privy Council opinion (which will no doubt in time be amended to a subsequent CFA decision), or conflicts with another prior decision of the Court of Appeal, or was made *per incuriam* (that is, made in ignorance of an authoritative rule of decisional law or statute which must, if considered, have led to a contrary result). There are several other situations where the court may escape the binding effect of its own decisions: flexibility is maintained despite a general obligation to be consistent.

Decisional law endeavours to be consistent because it is therefore predictable: social and economic life can be ordered by the law and reasonable expectations can be satisfied. And it would be highly inconvenient if previous decisions were not recognized as binding: every question would be open for re-argument, to the benefit perhaps of lawyers but to the detriment of society as a whole. Without consistency, people would not be treated equally. The law would run the risk of depending on individual whim, not on learning and the rational analysis of established doctrine. At the same time, however, judges attempt to preserve their freedom to amend the common law where it has obviously gone wrong or has become outdated. The tension between stability and creativity in decisional law is a fundamental characteristic of the system.

10. Statutes: Creation and Interpretation

IN Hong Kong, every ordinance is called a public ordinance. A *bill* (that is, proposed legislation which has been drafted and introduced into the legislative system, but not yet enacted), will be called a *private bill* if it provides primarily for the interests of individual persons or corporations, rather than those of the community at large, and is not a government measure; but the procedure in respect of it is not significantly different from the procedure for other bills. (A private bill's promoters, however, must pay a fee.) Ordinances, of which about eighty or ninety are passed each year, might make only minor amendments to prior ordinances, repeal and replace or consolidate predecessors, or provide for matters not previously covered by enacted law.

THE PROCESS OF LEGISLATION

There are various stages in the legislative process.

1. *Recognition of the need for legislation* — A problem has arisen in the existing law, perhaps perceived by a government lawyer or exposed by a recent judgment in the courts; a pressure group or responsible community opinion advocates abolition of harsh law or the enactment of new law to achieve a particular social purpose; a government department puts forward a policy requiring additional legal powers; the Hong Kong Law Reform Commission recommends change to the law. In all such cases a decision may be taken to draft a bill. The government of the SAR ('the executive authorities of the Region' (BL59)) is empowered to 'draft and introduce bills, motions and subordinate legislation' (BL62). Ultimate authority would normally come from the Executive Council if the bill is to be introduced by the government, but private bills may be promoted or adopted by a member of the Legislative Council without needing government approval. Similarly, bills not affecting the 'political structure or the operation of the government' and which do not call for public expenditure may be introduced by councillors, but the Chief Executive must give written consent for the introduction of bills relating to government policies (BL74).

2. *Drafting* — For government measures, instructions setting out the objects to be achieved are prepared and sent to the Drafting Division of the Department of Justice. A draftsman is assigned the task of composing the form of words in which the objects are to be realized. The draft is checked, revised if necessary, and sent to the Executive Council for approval.

3. *Consultation* — Sometimes, before ExCo sees the draft bill, copies will be sent to interested organizations and individuals for comment, perhaps resulting in further revisions of the draft.

4. *Notice of presentation* — Only members of LegCo may present a bill. A member must notify the Clerk of any intention to do so, and must attach to the bill an explanatory memorandum stating its contents and objects in non-technical language.

5. *Publication* — The Clerk will normally have the bill and its explanatory memorandum published in the government *Gazette* (Legal Supplement No. 3), thus giving notice to the public. Copies are also sent to every member of LegCo, and this constitutes presentation of the bill to the Council.

6. *First reading* — At a specified sitting of LegCo the short title of the bill is read by the Clerk. No debate is allowed, and the bill is ordered to be set down for second reading.

7. *Second reading* — On a motion that the bill be now read a second time there is a speech by the member in charge of the bill. Proceedings are then adjourned and the bill is usually referred to the House Committee, consisting of all members of LegCo. The House Committee may then pass the bill on to a Bills Committee (an *ad hoc* group formed to consider a particular bill), which considers its general merits, its detailed provisions, and whether it needs amendment. On return to and consideration by the House Committee the second reading debate is resumed.

8. *Committal* — If the second reading is agreed to, the bill is committed either to a committee of the whole Council or to a select committee. Such committees discuss the details of bills and may make amendments, provided notice is given. Each clause of a bill is considered in turn, then any schedules, and then the preamble (if there is one). The report of a select committee might be recommitted to a committee of the whole Council. After consideration by the larger group a bill is reported to the Council and is set down for its final reading.

9. *Third reading* — By this stage all the real work has been done. A motion is put that the bill be read a third time 'and do pass';

general speeches on the content of the bill may be made, and errors and oversights corrected, but no amendments of a material character may be proposed. When the motion is agreed to, the bill is considered to be passed, provided Annex II of the Basic Law has been complied with. Annex II requires that: (a) bills introduced by the government be passed by at least a simple majority of LegCo members present (there is a quorum of not less than one half of all LegCo members (BL75)); and (b) 'The passage of motions, bills or amendments to government bills introduced by individual members of the Legislative Council shall require a simple majority vote of each of the two groups of members present: members returned by functional constituencies and those returned by geographical constituencies through direct elections and by the Election Committee'. A bill which has been accordingly passed is then submitted by the Clerk to the Chief Executive for his signature.

10. *Chief Executive's signature and promulgation* — The CE, if he assents to the bill (which he is not obliged to do, though he is unlikely to refuse), signs it and 'promulgates' it. The bill becomes an ordinance on receiving the CE's signature, though it takes effect only after promulgation (BL76). 'Promulgation' is not a term which was familiar to the previous legal system; it appears to mean publication.

11. *Publication and commencement* — Normally every ordinance must be published in the *Gazette* (Legal Supplement No. 1). It comes into operation 'on the expiration of the day next preceding the day of such publication', so by the time a member of the public can buy copies from the Government Publications Centre the ordinance has been in operation since midnight of the previous day. Sometimes, however, an ordinance, or part of an ordinance, does not come into force until some later time notified in the *Gazette* or as specified in the ordinance itself.

12. *Reporting to the Standing Committee* — All ordinances must be reported to the Standing Committee of the NPC 'for the record', though this does not affect their entry into force (BL17). The Standing Committee may return an ordinance, though not amend it, if it considers the ordinance to be 'not in conformity with the provisions of [the Basic Law] regarding affairs within the responsibility of the Central Authorities and the Region' (BL17). Return has the effect of immediate invalidation, though without retroactive effect unless otherwise provided for by SAR law.

All these steps in the journey from draft bill to ordinance are designed to give opportunities for careful consideration of the wisdom of the proposed measure. The press can publicize it and provide a forum for public criticism; members of ExCo and LegCo can scrutinize it and debate it; and special interest groups can present their views. This does not necessarily ensure the absence of bad legislation, but the process no doubt prevents a fair amount of it from getting into the statute book. Yet hasty legislation is still possible: a new ordinance can complete all stages in one day if there is a need for urgency and if members of LegCo co-operate.

DELEGATED LEGISLATION

The expression 'subsidiary legislation', which in this respect is identical to 'delegated legislation' and 'subordinate legislation' (used in BL8), means any proclamation, rule, regulation, order, resolution, notice, rule of court, by-law, or other instrument made under or by virtue of any ordinance and having legislative effect. Power to make delegated legislation is conferred most often on executive officers, frequently the Chief Executive in Council (the Executive Council), and sometimes on outside bodies or judges. Such legislation is usually drafted in the Department of Justice, approved in ExCo, and published in the *Gazette* (Legal Supplement No. 2). All rules, regulations, by-laws, and so on must then be laid on the table of LegCo at its next sitting. LegCo may amend or revoke them by resolution. An ordinance may provide that subsidiary legislation shall be subject to approval by LegCo or some other authority, in which case the legislation must, of course, be submitted for approval and is subject to amendment by that body.

In England there are scrutiny committees in each House of Parliament whose job it is to review and report on delegated legislation. In Hong Kong the House Committee decides the manner of consideration of such legislation and may appoint sub-committees for the purpose.

Delegated legislation comes into force when published. Only rarely is there consultation with interested groups before it is made; it is not available in draft form prior to becoming law; and LegCo almost never debates it. Thus the safeguards which permit public opinion to be expressed on proposed primary legislation and which try to prevent careless lawmaking do not apply to delegated legislation. This is lawmaking by experts and, since it normally involves technical details rather than general principles, there are perhaps fewer reasons for requiring publicity and formal process through the legislature.

STATUTORY INTERPRETATION: GENERAL

It is a fundamental rule that judges must obey statutes. *Everyone* must obey statutes, which are superior as sources of law to decisional law, and thus whatever a competent legislature enacts must be accepted by judges and faithfully applied. Of course, the meaning of a statute must first be ascertained, and this is not always easy: legislators do not normally envisage every situation to which a statutory rule might be applicable, and the language they use is often ambiguous or its meaning subject to change over time. Determining meaning is a judicial task requiring considerable judgment and skill. Judges must not ascribe to a statute a meaning it cannot reasonably bear, for to do so would involve judges in the making of law, which is not supposed to be their role, and lead to their defiance of existing law to which they are subject in the same way as everyone else.

In fulfilling the interpretive function the judges must follow certain guidelines. Some of these are laid down by statute, some are part of decisional law.

STATUTORY RULES

Many ordinances contain definitions of important terms. The Interpretation and General Clauses Ordinance (cap. 1) contains over one hundred definitions and, unless a contrary intention can be discovered, these apply to all Hong Kong legislation. And in section 7 there are two additional rules: words and expressions importing the masculine gender include the female (a rule I have relied on in this book), and words and expressions in the singular include the plural and vice versa.

Cap. 1 also provides in section 19 a general principle for the interpretation of all ordinances:

An ordinance shall be deemed to be remedial and shall receive such fair, large and liberal construction and interpretation as will best ensure the attainment of the object of the Ordinance according to its true intent, meaning and spirit.

This provision itself, of course, needs interpreting. It does not say that genuine doubt as to the construction (or interpretation) of a statute should not be resolved in favour of an accused who would otherwise be punished, or that the literal meaning is not to be adopted, or even that the usual manner in which judges interpreted statutes before the section was enacted should not continue. But if the object of an ordinance is clear, and the words of a particular provision can fairly support a meaning which promotes that object, a judge may not interpret the words in a different sense.

COMMON LAW APPROACHES

It is often said that judges must find and give effect to the intention of the legislature: it is the legislature's job to enact law, and what the legislature intended in the enactment must be discerned and applied. But an equally important principle holds that all persons are entitled to rely on the law as it is enacted: it would be intolerable if law were other than what it plainly appears to be. And the intention of a legislature consisting of more than one person is often a myth. Different members of the legislature might well have had different ideas, or none at all, as to the meaning of the ordinances they voted for; one or two of them were probably asleep during much of the proceedings; perhaps only the draftsman knew clearly what was intended, and even he might have been confused by conflicting instructions. So the true principle is often said to be that judges must find and follow the intention of the legislature *as expressed in the words of the ordinance itself*. On this basis it is not appropriate for judges to ask the legislature what it intended or examine debates in the legislative chamber. Such a proceeding would only encourage legislators to be careless in the way they expressed themselves in statutes. Enacted law would not be autonomous and objective; we would be governed by legislators rather than by law.

Thus the traditional approach is to apply the words of a statute in their natural and ordinary sense. Their literal meaning is to be accepted even if unfortunate results occur; the duty of the court, said one Hong Kong judge, 'is not to make the law reasonable, but to expound it as it stands, according to the real sense of the words'.

STATUTES: CREATION AND INTERPRETATION   93

Thus additional words ought not to be read into an ordinance or existing words ignored. The clear language of an enactment must not be distorted in order to overcome hardship in a particular case. This approach was followed in relation to adoption, where the ordinance required the child to have been 'continuously in the care and possession of the applicant for at least six consecutive months immediately preceding the date of the order': though a boy had lived with an applicant from 1953 to 1961, he was at boarding-school in the United Kingdom when the adoption order was sought. He was therefore not in the applicant's care and possession, and could not be adopted.

The difficulty with the traditional approach is that words are infrequently precise and unambiguous. They will often bear an alternative meaning, one which in a particular case might seem more appropriate. It is not unreasonable to hold that a boy at boarding-school, entrusted by his guardians to the headmaster, remains within his guardians' 'care and possession'; certainly it is very doubtful if the legislature would have intended that such a boy should be incapable of being adopted. Judges have recognized a so-called 'golden rule' which permits them to avoid obvious absurdity or great inconvenience if a secondary meaning is available which leads to a more equitable result. Anomalies can thus be safely removed even if a less usual meaning of words is employed. Further, the House of Lords decided late in 1992 that in certain cases of ambiguity the courts may consult the words of the promoter of the statute when introducing it (in bill form) into the legislative chamber. This was a significant innovation which has been followed in Hong Kong. Indeed a sub-committee of the Law Reform Commission has recommended expansion of the situations where resort can be had to 'extrinsic aids' to interpretation (materials outside the actual terms of the legislation).

Another difficulty with the traditional approach is that the meaning of words often depends on the context in which they are used. That context is, or ought to be, the whole statute. Looked at in the isolation of the sentence in which they appear, the words 'care and possession' probably indicate to most people that a child should be actually living with the applicant who wishes to adopt. Taking the statute as a whole, however, the element of control through the choice of boarding-school and instructions to the headmaster might well be considered sufficient to constitute care and possession. Judges are justified in analyzing the ordinance in its entirety, seeking to understand its general objective or purpose, and interpreting particular words in relation to that purpose. An old formulation of the approach specified in section 19 of cap. 1 was in terms of the 'mischief' which the legislation was designed to cure: 'make such construction as shall suppress the mischief, and advance the remedy, . . . according to the true intent of the makers of the Act.' The more modern version is called the *purposive approach*: look for the overall purpose and give effect to it if that can be done without straining the words or violating the apparent intention of the legislature. This technique seems very similar to, or the same as, that required by section 19.

Lawyers used to talk of three different rules of statutory interpretation — the literal, golden, and mischief rules — and assume that judges could choose whichever rule suited their sense of justice in each case. This suggests that in reality judges were free to decide however they pleased, so long as their interpretations bore some relation to the statutory language, and that the guidelines placed no significant restraints on judicial discretion. If that were true, the notion of judges being bound by an ordinance would have little application. But, more recently, the courts have moved towards a fusion of the three rules and evolved a unitary approach. It is not just the letter of the law which is to be interpreted, as in the literal rule, or its spirit, as in the mischief rule, but both letter and spirit. The statutory context and the object of the legislation must at all times be considered; then anomalous results will be avoided or, if inescapable, regarded as intended and thus inevitable, for judges cannot change enacted law.

The interpretation of constitutional documents is often said to require a broader, more organic approach than the interpretation of ordinary statutes, involving greater flexibility and judicial statesmanship. This was accepted in 1992 as appropriate in regard to the Letters Patent (the colonial regime's principal constitutional document), and it would certainly seem apt in regard to the Basic Law. Several SAR judges have indeed applied it.

PRESUMPTIONS

It is well recognized that certain presumptions, long relied on by judges and thus known to and taken into account by legislators, can assist in the interpretation of statutes. These presumptions — which

STATUTES: CREATION AND INTERPRETATION 95

can be displaced by express statutory language — arise from judges' concepts of fairness or justice. Four examples will suffice, each illustrating how the general background of common law ideas can ameliorate the occasional inadvertent severity of enacted law.

1. *The presumption against strict liability* — Some offences can be committed whether the offender intended to do the act or not. At common law a person must intend to do a prohibited act, or be reckless or negligent in respect of it, before liability for the act arises, but statutes can create offences of strict liability, or 'absolute offences', where otherwise innocent behaviour leads to punishment. It is an offence, for example, to possess a forged travel document, but is a person guilty of this offence who sincerely and on good grounds believes his passport is genuine? 'No,' said a Hong Kong judge. 'When the legislature steps upon ground which involves the liberty of the subject it is treading sacred ground.' Some provisions which hitherto were thought to create absolute offences have fallen foul of the Bill of Rights.

2. *The presumption against the retrospective operation of statutes* — It is impossible to obey a statute which has not yet been enacted, except inadvertently, and law is brought into disrepute if it is applied to acts occurring before it comes into effect. Nevertheless, it is within the power of the legislature to make retroactive laws, though where substantive rights are affected, the intention is required by the courts to be unmistakable. The Bill of Rights has proved relevant in this area as well.

3. *The presumption against the exclusion of natural justice* — It is obviously unjust to allow decision-makers to be biased or to affect citizens' rights or interests without hearing them first, and the natural justice doctrine insists that decisions be impartially made and, in certain circumstances, subsequent to the grant of a hearing to affected persons. Even if an ordinance gives an administrator the authority to cancel a licence, for example, and makes no mention of any right to a hearing by the licence-holder, the courts often insist that cancellation of the licence is invalid unless such a hearing is given. A delegate lawmaker cannot dispense with the requirement to observe natural justice unless the authority to do so is clearly provided in the parent ordinance, and even the primary legislature may be inhibited in this respect by the Bill of Rights.

4. *The presumption against intending inconvenience or unreasonableness* — A regulation at Kai Tak airport, for example, created an offence for any unauthorized person to make an 'offer of

services' within the airport premises. Read literally, this would apply to a woman meeting a friend and offering to carry his bags. But no such interpretation was possible, said the judge: 'the intention which appears to be most in accordance with convenience, reason, justice and legal principles will, in all cases of doubtful significance, be presumed to be the true one.'

OTHER PRINCIPLES

There are other guidelines to which judges may refer. Most of these go under formidable Latin tags such as *generalia specialibus non derogant*, *expressio unius est exclusio alterius*, and *noscitur a sociis*. It is not necessary to explain them here: suffice it to recognize that the law of statutory interpretation is extensive and sophisticated. In theory it provides a basis for predicting how judges will construe legislation. Prediction cannot be certain, however, even where skilled lawyers are involved, and the process by which courts determine what lawmakers intended is never an automatic one.

11. Legal Personnel

WHO are the people who create and maintain law and administer the legal system? What roles do they play, and how are they appointed, educated, and organized?

THE CHIEF EXECUTIVE

The Chief Executive of Hong Kong is the most significant official in the constitutional apparatus of the territory: without his signature no ordinance can be promulgated, he is the head of the SAR (BL43) and of the executive branch (BL60), and he also has a modicum of quasi judicial authority in his power to appoint judges and pardon convicted persons or commute their penalties (BL48). He is not a merely formal figure like the monarch in the United Kingdom or the Governor-General of Australia. In Hong Kong the Chief Executive *is* the government (in formal terms the government is 'the executive authorities of the Region' (BL59), but all officials must of course obey him). He is not bound by the advice he receives from the Executive Council (BL56); and although he does not preside over the Legislative Council and has not the total control over its proceedings which the colonial Governor used to possess for most of the colonial period, he can probably still dominate the Council's proceedings. (See Chapter 4 on 'gubernatorial government'.)

In relation to the law, no bill can move from ExCo to LegCo without his approval. The drafting process, carried out in the Department of Justice, is subject to the CE's instructions. He, and he alone in Hong Kong, decides whether to assent to a bill presented to him after the third reading. As the CE in Council (the Executive Council) he makes much of the territory's subsidiary legislation. The enforcement of the law, by police and ICAC and administrative officials, is ultimately his responsibility. Under the Emergency Regulations Ordinance he is given extremely wide powers to deal with situations of emergency or public danger. He may not interfere with the way judges and magistrates carry out their functions, but through his power to pardon and commute he can interfere with judicial activity after the event.

He is, in one sense perhaps, a servant of the government in Beijing, which appoints him (he is 'accountable to the Central People's Government' (BL43) though also to the SAR), but the 'high degree of autonomy' granted to the SAR is inconsistent with regular instructions passing from the Central People's Government to the CE. In practice he does not and could not personally intervene in every detail of the lawmaking and law-enforcement processes. It would be unconstitutional for him to instruct the Secretary for Justice in the decision whether to prosecute suspected offenders (see BL63) or the Commissioner of the ICAC in investigating allegations of corruption (although the Commission is accountable to him (BL58)), and he may not suspend the operation of law generally or dispense with it in particular cases. Like every other citizen he must obey the law, even if he made it himself, and he may be sued or prosecuted in the courts if he acts illegally. Nevertheless, the CE is pre-eminent in the non-judicial portion of the legal system. (See Chapter 4 for details of his selection.)

LEGISLATORS

The Legislative Council 'shall be the legislature of the Region' (BL66). As such it considers and passes bills, but it cannot bring them into operation without the co-operation of the Chief Executive (BL76). The 'first Legislative Council' (not to be confused with the Provisional Legislative Council 1997–8 which, although it was the first legislature in fact, was not the 'first LegCo' as that term is used in various NPC decisions prior to 1 July 1997) comprises sixty members elected for a two-year term. They are elected either by:

1. geographical constituencies through direct elections (twenty members);
2. functional constituencies (thirty members); or
3. the Election Committee (ten members).

At least 80 per cent of members must be Chinese citizens who are permanent residents of the SAR with no right of abode in any foreign country; the remaining members must be permanent residents though not necessarily of Chinese nationality or without a foreign right of abode (BL67). Candidates for election were required to uphold the Basic Law and pledge allegiance to the SAR. From the year 2000 onwards elections are to be held every four years.

Traditionally in Hong Kong the government had an assured majority in LegCo: half the members held office under the Crown and were obliged to vote with the government, and the Governor had a casting vote in the unlikely event of a tied house. The non-government appointees never attempted to act as a united opposition party, and even when non-government appointed and elected members attained a majority they could not cause the government to lose office and they did not seek to do so. With the institution in 1991 of direct elections to LegCo on a geographical basis, the Council began to look more like its counterpart in a parliamentary democracy. The legislature elected in 1995 was denounced by mainland Chinese officials as having been created inconsistently with the Basic Law and the principle of 'convergence'. Nevertheless it operated for two years and was a lively body of divergent interests which could not be described as subservient to the executive government. The Provisional Legislative Council which replaced it (until new elections in June 1998) had a rather limited role and was composed of members not disposed to challenge Tung Chee-hwa's administration. The first LegCo of the SAR has not, at the time of writing, been elected, but arrangements for the electoral process are likely to produce a more quiescent body than the last colonial legislature.

LEGAL OFFICERS

The Legal Aid and Registrar General's Departments employ a number of lawyers to administer and advise, but the majority of government lawyers belong to the Department of Justice. Some of these, under the Law Draftsman, prepare the bills which are submitted to LegCo and the subsidiary legislation enacted under powers delegated by ordinance; others, under the Law Officer (Civil Law), undertake the government's civil litigation work and advise other government departments. Perhaps better known are the prosecutors, who conduct criminal trials and appeals and are consulted by the police and other law enforcement agencies. The Director of Public Prosecutions is at the top of the Prosecutions

Division, while the Solicitor General is in charge of the Legal Policy Division (which houses the secretariat of the Hong Kong Law Reform Commission). Also in the department is the International Law Division, which handles international agreements and matters such as international legal assistance.

The Department of Justice, formerly the Legal Department (also known as the Attorney General's Chambers), is headed by the Secretary for Justice, who is head of the Hong Kong Bar, Chairman of the Law Reform Commission, Protector of Charities, and much more besides. The present incumbent sits on the Executive Council. No official is more important to the administration of justice than the Secretary for Justice. She is responsible for the varied operations of her chambers, and in particular the ultimate decisions on deployment of the criminal law rest with her and her alone: no one, not even the CE (whom she advises), can instruct her whether to prosecute any individual (BL63). As the government's principal legal adviser she can influence every part of the legal system except the judiciary, and even there she has a say through her membership of the Judicial Officers Recommendation Commission and in appointments to the Bench. She also has a right of audience in every court. Any doubts in the integrity of the Secretary for Justice would impair confidence in the entire process of law-making and law administration.

In 1991, the office of Official Solicitor was created. The Official Solicitor's duties include acting for certain persons as guardian in court proceedings or on behalf of persons committed to prison for contempt who do not seek release, as guardian of an infant related to a person subject to the Mental Health Ordinance, or for any party involved in proceedings for the care and protection of a juvenile.

LAWYERS

Most people would agree that lawyers are a regrettable necessity: necessary because the law is too voluminous and complex to be understood and utilized by individuals without legal training, regrettable because they are usually expensive. Their role is to resolve conflicts (as where persons are accused of criminal offences or civil wrongs), to facilitate transactions (by drawing up contracts, for example, or wills), and to assist in providing order and security for the future (by drafting legislation, promoting fairness in official life, and challenging abuses of power). The services they provide are essential to modern society. In particular, lawyers in private practice are independent of the government and can initiate action against officialdom or defend citizens against arbitrary interference with their rights. They are thus important to maintenance of the rule of law; an independent judiciary would be largely meaningless without a strong legal profession.

The private profession of lawyers consists of the two separate branches of barristers and solicitors. Barristers, who in England are historically the senior side of the profession, are specialists in advocacy and legal advice: they appear in the courts on behalf of clients, they prepare certain documents relating to litigation, and they advise on the law in conference with solicitor and client and through written opinions. Solicitors, on the other hand, tend to do more of the paperwork: property transfers, lease agreements, divorce arrangements, contracts, and so on. But solicitors often do the same kind of work as barristers, for they also advise on the law, represent clients (in the lower courts and in negotiations with other parties), and assist in litigation. So far as members of the public are concerned, solicitors are usually the only kind of lawyer whose services they need. If you buy a flat, or make a will, or are in disagreement with your landlord, or are accused of a minor crime, it is a solicitor whom you may want to consult. A barrister will normally be desired only if the legal issue is particularly complicated or if the case goes to the District Court or above. He may be retained only through a solicitor. Solicitors may be appointed (by the Chief Justice) as notaries public, with powers to attest and authenticate documents and to administer oaths, affirmations, or declarations.

The academic training of lawyers in Hong Kong is the same for both solicitors and barristers. All intending lawyers must first obtain a law degree (LLB) from the University of Hong Kong or the City University, or a Common Professional Examination Certificate if they are already graduates in a non-law discipline, and then a Postgraduate Certificate in Laws (PCLL). The PCLL is awarded after one year of study at one of the universities. The whole period of study occupies four years and is followed by a term of apprenticeship: two years as a trainee with a solicitors' firm to become a solicitor, or one year of pupillage which a novice barrister spends in the chambers of a barrister of at least five years' standing. After completion of traineeship (formerly called 'articles'), during which extra courses of study ('continuing professional development') are required, a person may be admitted as a solicitor. A person may be admitted as a barrister before embarking on pupillage, but may not qualify to practise as such until pupillage is completed. Solicitors may not practise on their own account or in partnership until after two years employment with an established solicitor in Hong Kong.

Solicitors may join firms either as salaried personnel or as partners. They deal directly with lay clients (the individuals or organizations who seek their services) and instruct barristers if further advice or assistance is needed. Barristers may not, however, enter into partnership with one another: they are genuinely self-employed, though usually in association with other barristers in a set of chambers which enables them to share overheads like rent, secretarial services, and library facilities. Generally, they may not see clients in the absence of a solicitor, and they cannot sue for their fees. The rationale for such restrictions on a barrister's practice is unclear, but, whatever the reasons, barristers are individualists who might on that account be more independent than solicitors: that is, they might be less vulnerable to being influenced by others (they have no employers or senior partners to instruct them) and thus might be more ready to represent persons whose cause is unpopular or politically disfavoured. Whether this is so or not, barristers tend to enjoy slightly higher prestige than solicitors: only barristers can become Senior Counsel, and it is from their ranks that judges are normally appointed (though the monopoly they once enjoyed in this respect has recently been abolished).

One criterion often required of a profession is that it is self-organized with internal powers of discipline. In this respect solicitors and barristers belong to separate professions. Solicitors are under the control of the Law Society, whose Council makes rules (under the Legal Practitioners Ordinance) regulating such matters as the conduct and discipline of solicitors, the issue of practising certificates, and traineeship and exams. Since 1992, disciplinary tribunals, which after inquiry or investigation may impose censure or monetary penalties, suspend solicitors, or strike them off the roll, are composed of two solicitors and one lay person; members are appointed by the tribunal convenor (a solicitor) from a panel appointed by the Chief Justice. Similar arrangements have been made for the investigation of complaints against barristers. Appeals go to the Court of Appeal, and aggrieved practitioners could probably also seek judicial review from the Court of First Instance. Whether behaviour amounts to misconduct or not is largely determined by rules set down by the professions themselves.

Lawyers thus constitute a divided profession, the two branches (or separate professions) working in close co-operation but under different rules regarding admission, areas of specialization, and organization and control. In some other common law countries, such as the United States of America and Singapore, there is a fused or amalgamated profession: a lawyer is simply a lawyer, able to combine the functions of both solicitor and barrister. This system is often said to be more efficient, cheaper, and more conducive to confidence between lawyer and client than the system which prevails in Hong Kong. Against this, it is argued that division better ensures the availability of advocates, promotes the acquisition of specialist knowledge and skills, encourages a more objective view of the lay client's case, advances ethical integrity, and does not necessarily lead to less efficiency or greater expense. In the first edition of this book it was opined that there is a good deal of vested interest and professional inertia affecting the debate on this issue and that it was not likely that 'fusion' would be attempted during the foreseeable future. In 1993, however, the Law Society proposed the creation of a mixed system whereby individual lawyers could choose whether to act purely as solicitors, purely as barristers, or as both. Apprenticeship would be the same for all intending lawyers: those specializing in advocacy, who now become barristers, could if they wished join firms of lawyers while continuing to offer specialist advocacy skills; those who maintained a primarily solicitor's practice would be eligible for appointment to the Bench. The Bar, however, opposed this proposal, and it was not implemented. Nevertheless certain reforms have been made: solicitors can now be appointed as judges, in some limited situations barristers can consult with clients (such as employed barristers, accountants, arbitrators, and company secretaries) without the mediation of a solicitor, and barristers may appear in the courts without a solicitor if no prejudice to the interests of the client or of justice generally is thereby caused. The two-counsel rule, which required a Senior Counsel to be accompanied by a junior colleague, has been abolished. The Law Society has considerably relaxed restrictions on advertising by solicitors. But other proposed reforms have not, or not yet, been implemented: solicitors have not achieved their goal of acquiring rights of audience in the higher courts, barristers may still not enter into a contract for their services, 'conditional fees' (a proportion of any award in a civil action) are not permitted, multidisciplinary practices in which solicitors join in a firm with other professionals such as accountants appear not to have happened, the capacity of solicitors' firms to incorporate, though created by legislation, awaits implementing rules, and so on.

In 1985, there were over 2,100 lawyers in Hong Kong, with over three hundred of them working for the government; in 1992, 3,908 practising certificates were issued and 248 persons were employed at the Crown Counsel grade in the Attorney General's Chambers. (These figures do not take account of foreign lawyers who do not practise Hong Kong law but advise on the law of other countries or assist in the raising of money on the international market.) Of the 1,795 in private practice in 1985, 1,518 were solicitors and 277 were barristers. By 1992, 2,721 solicitors and 487 barristers held practising certificates; women comprised 28.3 per cent of the solicitors as opposed to just 16 per cent of the barristers. In early 1998 the figures were: practising barristers: 669 (83 per cent male); solicitors in private practice: 4,233; in-house lawyers (including government lawyers): 469; foreign law firms: 52. Hong Kong had 34 private lawyers per 100,000 persons in 1986 whereas Singapore had 50, New Zealand 100, and England and Wales 110. In 1993, the corresponding figure for Hong Kong was 55, whereas in 1998 it appears to have risen to 79. Since 1987, there have been 150 students in the first year of the LLB curriculum at the University of Hong Kong, and since 1988 a further 60 have entered the law course at the City Polytechnic or University. Foreign lawyers (including now those trained in or qualified to practise in the United Kingdom) can take an examination and then practise here. This great expansion of the profession may eventually mean that legal needs currently unmet will be provided for and legal services will become less expensive. There is a curious rule of legal sociology, however, which may stand in the way of these desirable objectives: legal work tends to expand to suit the interests of the lawyers available to do it. This is known as Wesley-Smith's Law. It is currently under pressure, and some unemployed lawyers even doubt its validity.

In 1988, a working party chaired by the Chief Justice recommended various measures for licensing foreign law firms and foreign lawyers, and several US firms petitioned the Governor for permission to employ Hong Kong solicitors or admit them as partners and for the right of foreign lawyers to be admitted to practise as barristers or solicitors without examination. The Law Society expressed furious opposition. However, foreign lawyers, foreign law firms, and associations between Hong Kong firms and foreign law firms may now be registered in accordance with the Legal Practitioners Ordinance. The foreign lawyers may not practise Hong Kong law; however, persons with qualifications acquired outside Hong Kong can in certain circumstances, and under the control of the Council of the Law Society, be admitted as solicitors, though examinations on Hong Kong law and practice must be passed before admission.

Hong Kong, as a member of the General Agreement on Trade in Services (GATS), is committed to ensuring that admissions requirements for lawyers are objective, reasonable, and standards-based, thus promoting the liberalization and expansion of trade in services. The Law Society has significantly changed its rules in order to meet this obligation. The Bar, however, has not. It is very difficult for an overseas lawyer to practise in Hong Kong as a barrister: there is no examination she can sit to 'localize' her qualifications, lengthy residence requirements are still in place, and discrimination based on geographical origin or place of overseas admission continues to exist.

JUDGES AND MAGISTRATES

There are three permanent judges in the Court of Final Appeal in addition to the Chief Justice and panels of non-permanent Hong Kong judges and judges from other common law jurisdictions. Nine Justices of Appeal sit in the Court of Appeal and twenty-five judges in the Court of First Instance, and there are thirty-three District Judges as well as a Chief District Judge, a President (a CFI judge) in the Lands Tribunal with two Presiding Officers (District Judges) and two surveyors as members, six adjudicators in the Small Claims Tribunal, eight presiding officers in the Labour Tribunal, three posts of coroner, two presiding magistrates in the Obscene Articles Tribunal, and a Chief Magistrate, ten Principal Magistrates, and fifty-one permanent magistrates. At their head is the Chief Justice of the CFA who, assisted by registrars and the Judiciary Administrator, is responsible for judicial administration. The total number of cases filed before the regular courts in 1996 (excluding the CFA, which was not then established) exceeded 630,000 (1,586 in the Court of Appeal, 34,485 in the then High Court, 49,084 in the District Court, and over 550,000 in the magistracies). Before the Labour Tribunal 7,862 cases were filed, the Small Claims Tribunal heard 17,445 claims, the Obscene Articles Tribunal considered 1,212 applications for classification of materials, and there were 201 death inquiries by coroners and 2,287 concluded cases in the Lands Tribunal.

All judicial officers are appointed by the Chief Executive (formerly by the Governor) or, by delegation in respect of lower levels, the Chief Justice. In this task he is advised by the Judicial Officers Recommendation Commission (formerly the Judicial Service Commission), a body chaired by the Chief Justice and including the Secretary for Justice and seven other members appointed by the CE (two of them judges, one a barrister, one a solicitor, and three lay persons). The Commission's role is not purely advisory (BL88 — judges shall be appointed by the CE *on the recommendation of* an independent commission — appears to mean that recommendations must be accepted), and its deliberations, which may include the consideration of representations made by judges and magistrates regarding their conditions of service, are strictly confidential.

No particular qualifications are required of magistrates, though in practice all permanent magistrates are legally qualified. Special magistrates, who are not lawyers and whose jurisdiction and powers are very limited, may be appointed. Magistrates are, in a sense, in the front line of judicial work: they often operate without the benefit of lawyers appearing before them, they have to keep a record of all proceedings in their courts, juries do not assist them in determining the facts, they hear a great many cases (usually well over half a million per year), and their 'clients' (the accused persons) are often poor, socially disadvantaged, and bewildered by the whole process. Special qualities of patience, sympathy, courtesy, and fairness are demanded of magistrates (and, indeed, of all judicial personnel).

The higher one goes up the court hierarchy, the greater are the qualifications or experience required. A District Judge must have been a practising lawyer for at least five years. To become a judge of the Court of first Instance a person must have had ten years' experience as a lawyer, magistrate, or District Judge. For appointment to either court the appointee may alternatively have served for the appropriate period in the Attorney General's Chambers or Department of Justice, Registrar General's Department, or Legal Aid Department, or, during the colonial period, have been a member of the Colonial Legal Service, the Legal Branch of Her Majesty's Overseas Civil Service, or Her Majesty's Overseas Judiciary. Hong Kong has recruited many of its judges either from the government or from the ranks of career judges in British colonies. The judiciary as a whole is sometimes criticized as a civil service judiciary, for two reasons: many judges have spent most of their earlier careers not in private practice but in serving government, and a common pattern of promotion from the lower to the higher courts has emerged. This leads to unproven suspicions that some judges — whose advancement formerly depended upon the approval of the Governor — have been unwilling to avoid subservience to government interests. The common practice of elevating to the Bench government lawyers, who may have spent most of their professional lives as prosecutors, is in this respect particularly unfortunate, though the reluctance of successful private practitioners to accept judicial appointment has probably left the administration no real alternative. Since 1973, however, the private Bar has supplied a good number of judges to the District Court and above, and others have become magistrates; in 1992, a local QC joined the Court of Appeal, and this has perhaps encouraged other practitioners to seek appointment to the higher courts. (The current Chief Justice of the Court of Final Appeal and the three permanent judges of that court were all previously Senior Counsel in private practice.) Localization at the lower levels of the judiciary has been considerably enhanced over the last few years. In February 1993, the Chief Justice claimed that 40 per cent of the judges and magistrates in post were locals, and the percentage has risen since then.

The even-handed administration of justice, the impartial application of law without fear or favour, the dispassionate analysis of facts and legal arguments to achieve the correct result, commitment to the spirit of legality: such are the expectations we have of our judges. In short, judges are supposed to be *independent* — and are required by BL85 to be so. This means, in particular, independence from the executive government: as an Attorney General in Hong Kong once said, it would be a 'constitutional outrage' for the judges to receive instructions from ExCo. Judges must, of course, obey the legislature (they are faithful to the law), but not individual legislators; even the CE, once he has appointed them, cannot tell them what to do. Assisted by an independent legal profession, an independent judiciary ensures that private citizens have no formal disadvantage in legal proceedings against other parties who are wealthier, socially more prominent, or politically more powerful. This is not to deny, however, that judges, and through them the law, tend towards conservative ideas. A former Chief Justice, Sir Denys Roberts, once pointed out the obvious fact that:

> Generally a judge is middle-aged and, by comparison with most of society, well paid and enjoying a comfortable middle class standard of living. His ways of thought and pattern of life, even assuming, as is usually not yet the case in Hong Kong, that he is of the same race as the defendants, are very different from theirs.

The independence of the judges is supported by several institutional arrangements:

1. *Security of tenure* — a judge of the Supreme Court or a District Judge holds office until he or she reaches the retirement age and cannot be removed from the post except for inability to discharge the functions of office or for misbehaviour. Dismissal of such judges other than the Chief Justice of the Court of Final Appeal can only occur if a tribunal of fellow local judges, appointed by the Chief Justice, so recommends. (Formerly the matter had to be referred to the Judicial Committee of the Privy Council, and only if that Committee so advised the Queen was the judge dismissed. This never happened in pre-1997 Hong Kong.) The Chief Justice may be investigated by a tribunal, appointed by the CE, of at least five local judges (BL89). He and the Chief Judge of the High Court may not be removed without the endorsement of the Legislative Council (BL90). Under the Judicial Officers (Tenure of Office) Ordinance a judicial officer lower in the hierarchy than a District Judge is liable to dismissal for inability to discharge duties or misbehaviour after inquiry by the Chief Justice, investigation by a tribunal of two High Court judges and a public officer, report to the Judicial Officers Recommendation Commission, and recommendation to the Chief Executive. This applies to all magistrates, members of tribunals, registrars, etc. appointed on permanent terms and to officers employed on agreement terms after three years of employment. BL91 requires the SAR to maintain the previous system of appointment and removal of 'members of the judiciary other than judges' (though it is not clear to whom this refers). No judge has been dismissed in Hong Kong since security of tenure was intro-

duced, but several have resigned following allegations about their professional conduct.

2. *Adequate remuneration* — Judges are well paid and for that reason should not be susceptible to bribery. This is a principle which, unsurprisingly, is strongly supported by the judges themselves, magistrates in particular often complaining that their salaries are much too low (though considerably improved since the first edition of this book). BL93 requires that judges serving in Hong Kong pre-1997 continue in employment with pay, allowances, benefits, and conditions of service no less favourable than before, and on retirement or resignation judicial pensions, gratuities, allowances, and benefits shall not be reduced. Judicial pensions are a right guaranteed by ordinance.

3. *Appointment* — The role of the Judicial Officers Recommendation Commission is to advise on the best candidates to fill judicial vacancies and not to favour persons who seem most likely to side with the government. The former rule (of its predecessor, the Judicial Service Commission) that its advice must be unanimous was probably designed to counter the influence of the government personnel who sat on it, but now the Secretary for Justice is the only member representing the executive branch, and the Commission's resolutions are effective even if up to two members vote against them. The CE may not be free to reject the Commission's recommendations (as discussed above).

4. *Immunity* — No legal action can be taken against judges personally for things done or said in the exercise of their judicial functions (this is a common law principle, reinforced by BL85).

5. *Power to punish for contempt* — Behaviour which improperly seeks to deflect a judge from the impartial administration of justice can be dealt with by imprisonment for contempt of court.

6. *Fancy dress* — The wigs and gowns worn by judges, combined with the architecture of the courtroom and the solemnity with which proceedings are conducted, are calculated to impress observers with the majesty of the law and the impartiality of its judicial stewardship. Unfortunately they can also lead to judicial pomposity.

7. *Convention of the constitution* — It is a well-established convention, generally respected in Hong Kong, that no government official may attempt to interfere in the judicial process. Even criticism in LegCo would be out of order.

8. *Institutional autonomy* — The Chief Justice of Court of Final Appeal is responsible for administration of the courts, assisted by

the Judiciary Administrator, the registrars, and court leaders at each level. The Judiciary Administrator co-ordinates preparation of the annual budget and negotiates it with the Financial Secretary and committees of legislators. Thus the executive branch of government has no control over the day-to-day operations of the courts.

Some interesting statistics compiled on 319 judges and magistrates appointed or in office during the years 1950 to 1990 reveal that:

- Only 21 per cent were local, in the sense that they were born in Hong Kong or China and educated here; of these 80 per cent had Chinese names. Britons made up 48 per cent of the total.
- Women represented just 6 per cent, though the rate of appointment of women has increased dramatically in recent years.
- Those that had had previous experience as professional prosecutors made up 38 per cent.
- Many judicial personnel had had experience in Commonwealth jurisdictions outside their place of qualification.
- Of those that studied law, 25 per cent had qualified as solicitors, 60 per cent as barristers, and 15 per cent as both in a fused profession.

It would be unprofitable to speculate as to the influence that nationality, gender, service with the government, experience in other jurisdictions, and type of legal training might have on judicial performance, but it may be surmised that such factors are not irrelevant. We lack the means to measure them with sufficient accuracy.

Confidence in the impartiality and independence of the judiciary is a precious thing: without it the whole legal system, and its objective of the rule of law, would be at risk and the social, political, and economic health of the territory would be diminished.

JUSTICES OF THE PEACE

The Chief Executive may appoint Justices of the Peace (JPs), and several hundred citizens of Hong Kong occupy that office. Some are designated New Territories JPs. Early in the colony's history, JPs played an active role in the administration of justice at the lowest level, but now their functions are few (though not necessarily unimportant): they administer oaths and declarations, visit prisons and report on prison conditions, and serve on advisory panels. New Territories JPs are members of the Full Council of the Heung Yee Kuk.

ACADEMICS

The final category of legal personnel worthy of mention comprises the teachers of law at the universities. As imparters of information about law, and of attitudes, techniques, and values, they play an important role in the legal system. Just as significant is their duty to carry out research and, exploiting the concept of academic freedom, to monitor, comment on, and if necessary criticize the performance of the legal system.

12. Other Aspects of the Legal System

JURIES

Adjudication in a civil dispute, or when a criminal charge is laid against a person, involves two main tasks: determining the facts and deciding upon the appropriate law (followed, at least in theory, by the application of the law to the facts to reach a result). Choosing the law can best be performed by personnel who are legally trained, and judges fulfil that function. In many cases they make findings of fact as well, but in serious criminal cases it is desirable that fact-finding be the preserve of juries. Thus criminal trials in the Court of First Instance — though not at present in any other courts — are conducted before a judge and jury. In some civil cases, too, such as actions for defamation or malicious prosecution, a party may elect to have issues of fact tried by a jury.

In England it is traditionally said that a jury consists of 'twelve good men and true'. In Hong Kong the jury consists of seven (sometimes nine) good and true men and women, not being infirm or under 21 or over 65 years of age, who understand sufficient English and are resident in the territory. All such persons are liable for jury service, though certain categories (such as members of LegCo or the spouses of High Court judges) are exempt. The function of the jury in civil cases is to decide questions of fact which are contested by the parties, and at least a simple majority of jurors (four out of seven) is required. In criminal cases the jury answers the question: 'Guilty or not guilty?' A majority of five jurors is sufficient for a verdict.

In choosing between guilty and not guilty the jury determines the facts (for example: 'Was the accused at the scene of the murder? Did he hold the knife which stabbed the victim?'), and applies the law as explained by the judge (for example: 'Did the accused act in self-defence? Was he provoked or insane?'). The jury's deliberations are conducted in secret and free from any pressure, and reasons are not required; jurors can therefore, if they wish, refuse to convict an accused even though it is clear that he committed the act without lawful excuse. This is not necessarily improper, and indeed the capacity of the jury to refuse to convict is the reason

OTHER ASPECTS OF THE LEGAL SYSTEM 113

why juries are often regarded as exercising a vital constitutional function in defence of individual liberty. Jurors who believe a law to be thoroughly bad, or a prosecution to be oppressive, or an accused to be morally (though not legally) justified in his criminal act, can deliver a verdict of not guilty, thus letting the Secretary for Justice know that a random sample of Hong Kong citizens disapprove of her action in bringing the accused person to trial. The jury system permits a severe law to be mitigated in particular cases. It also involves ordinary people, with no legal expertise, in the administration of justice and assures a defendant that his case is not disposed of entirely by officials.

This is not to say that the jury system does not have its defects. It is expensive, both in extending the length of trials and in providing fees to jurors, and jury service is inevitably unpopular with many of the people who are obliged to sit. The language requirement ensures that, usually, only middle-class persons serve on juries — though the high level of education enjoyed by the average juror may be regarded as a strength of the Hong Kong system. Nevertheless, in some cases, such as complex commercial crimes trials, the evidence may be just too complicated and extensive for ordinary people to understand. This consideration prompted the government to propose in 1985 that juries be replaced in such cases by assessors with special knowledge of the commercial world. Public opinion, however, strongly favoured retention of the jury system whenever an alleged criminal is charged with a serious offence. Indeed, it has been proposed that jury trials be introduced into the District Court, though the prospect of this occurring seems remote. The Basic Law provides that 'The principle of trial by jury previously practised in Hong Kong shall be maintained' (BL86).

LEGAL AID, ADVICE, AND ASSISTANCE

If the complexities of law make lawyers indispensable, and if lawyers are expensive, 'going to law' must be well beyond the means of many Hong Kong people. Yet without legal representation a litigant is severely disadvantaged: even the routine of a lawyer's practice, such as issuing writs, preparing statements of claim, and seeking discovery, can be understood and carried out by few who are not lawyers. The rules of evidence and procedure are sophisticated; the art of advocacy does not come easily. The courts, accustomed to the adversarial system, rely on each party presenting his or her own case in the proper form, and though judges have a duty to assist an unrepresented party, lay persons can rarely do as well in court as lawyers can. It would be unjust if they were denied professional assistance because of purely financial considerations. Thus various schemes exist to help those who cannot afford lawyers (and, it must be admitted, to help lawyers who might otherwise have few clients). Foremost among these schemes is the system of *legal aid* run by the Legal Aid Department and funded by the government. If a person's financial resources are less than certain limits (currently $169,700 after deduction of prescribed allowances), and in civil cases there is in addition a reasonable chance of success in the action, legal aid will be granted. This means that a lawyer (or lawyers) will be provided free or on payment of a small contribution. Most accused persons in the District Court and above are legally aided, though the scheme does not cover the magistracies except for committal proceedings. Criminal appeals attract legal aid if there are arguable grounds of appeal, and in murder cases legal aid is always available.

Many people (belonging to 'the sandwich class') are too poor to hire lawyers for themselves, yet too wealthy to qualify for legal aid. In personal injuries and fatal accidents cases, and certain claims for professional negligence, such persons can receive legal aid on condition that they pay a registration fee and contribute back a percentage of any damages awarded. Since July 1992 there has been a significant increase in the number of people who qualify for legal aid; in 1997 15,702 legal aid certificates in civil cases were granted, compared to just 9,134 the previous year and 7,516 in 1995. The civil applications in 1997 were dominated by matrimonial cases (41.8 per cent). Over 35 per cent of criminal applications were for trial in the District Court.

If rule of law objectives are to be met, it is important that legal aid be administered independently of the executive government, particularly as some recipients of legal aid are involved in legal action against government officials or departments. Yet the Legal Aid Department is itself a department of government. The possibility of a conflict of interest thus arising has prompted calls for the privatization of legal aid, with the scheme being administered by the private legal profession. These calls were rejected by ExCo in 1990, though they were renewed in 1993 by the legal profession. A thorough review of legal aid services was conducted in 1992–4 and,

OTHER ASPECTS OF THE LEGAL SYSTEM

as a result, the Legal Aid Services Council was established in 1996. The Council's functions include the formulation of policies governing the provision of legal aid by the Legal Aid Department, regular review of the work, services, and development plans of the Department, and the provision of advice to the Chief Executive on government policy concerning legal aid services. One matter on which the Council is expressly authorized to advise is the feasibility and desirability of establishing an independent legal aid authority, which might, as the legal profession had supported, involve terminating the Legal Aid Department and creating a new body separate from the civil service. The Council, which though funded by government is an independent body, has not yet (1998) made any recommendation on the legal aid authority.

In addition to the services provided by the Legal Aid Department, there is a *duty lawyer* scheme which assigns barristers and solicitors to the magistracies. Lawyers on duty give 'on-the-spot' advice and representation for accused persons. The scheme was considerably expanded in 1991. Free legal advice is also given in the evenings by volunteer (unpaid) lawyers at offices in various locations around the urban areas. This scheme, like that of duty lawyers, is administered by the Law Society and the Bar Association and is financed by the government. Another service enables people to listen to recordings giving legal information over the telephone.

THE BILL OF RIGHTS

In 1991 the Hong Kong Bill of Rights Ordinance was passed, representing a departure for the legal system: for the first time in Hong Kong various fundamental rights and freedoms were laid down which the courts were authorized to enforce through the interpretation and review of statutes. The Bill of Rights consists of twenty-three articles reproduced from the International Covenant on Civil and Political Rights (ICCPR), an international treaty which sought to implement the Universal Declaration of Human Rights. Each article sets out in broad terms a basic right or freedom: to life, to liberty and security of person, to speech, thought, conscience, and religion, to equality before the law, and so forth, though subject to certain qualifications and reservations. Pre-existing legislation which infringed these declarations of rights could be struck down to the extent of their inconsistency. Subsequent legislation, which on general principle cannot normally be controlled by an ordinary enactment, could in effect also be regulated by the Bill of Rights through a provision inserted into the colonial constitution. This device was designed to operate also under BL39, which states that the ICCPR as applied to Hong Kong 'shall remain in force and shall be implemented through the laws of the HKSAR' and that restrictions to rights and freedoms shall not contravene the continuation in force of the ICCPR. Accordingly, if the design is effective, the Bill of Rights is a standard against which all legislation can be measured and, if found wanting, rendered inoperative so far as it interferes with our rights. The mainland authorities were not impressed by the bill of rights ordinance, but allowed it to survive the transition to Chinese rule subject to certain amendments. These amendments are unlikely to affect the operation of the Bill of Rights in the SAR in any significant way.

The courts have generally responded to the Bill of Rights with some caution. Thus the Bill's impact on the legal system has been rather small, though in some cases decisive, and the document has no doubt deterred legislators from passing legislation which would be vulnerable to challenge under its provisions. Chapter III of the Basic Law also seeks to protect rights and freedoms, though it will probably prove less valuable in this respect. The Bill of Rights provides citizens with a method of claiming rights against the government and thus controlling government action, and this is of at least symbolic significance.

LAW REFORM

In England there is a Law Commission charged with keeping the law under review and attending to its systematic development and reform. Hong Kong's efforts in regard to law reform are more modest, and indeed until relatively recently they were virtually non-existent. But there is now a Law Reform Commission which considers topics referred to it by the Secretary for Justice or the Chief Justice and makes recommendations on how the law can be improved. It is, of course, merely advisory, and it relies on the unpaid labours of many lawyers, academics, and public-spirited citizens.

THE LANGUAGE OF THE LAW

There is a presumption that everyone knows the law. Of course, no one *does* know *all* the law, not even judges of the Court of Final Appeal, and very few people are experts. But justice requires that everyone have a reasonable opportunity to find out the law, and not solely by consulting lawyers. Law made in Hong Kong should therefore be available in Chinese and legal proceedings should, wherever appropriate, be conducted in Chinese as well. The Basic Law (BL9) provides that English may be used in addition to Chinese as an official language by the judiciary of the Special Administrative Region, which seems to make reform a constitutional requirement.

It is a remarkable fact that, until recently, most trials in Hong Kong were conducted in, and nearly all law was published in, a language which is not the mother tongue of 98 per cent of the inhabitants. The language of the law is still largely English (even the Official Languages Ordinance, which made Chinese an official language, was passed in English only — though there is now a Chinese version). The District Court and the Court of First Instance function predominantly in English (apart from Latin and Law French). Magistrates are permitted to use Chinese, but some cannot and do not. Officials of the Labour and Small Claims Tribunals can and do, when the parties are Chinese, but these, and increasingly the magistracies, are the only major judicial forums in which the Chinese (Cantonese) language is regularly employed. However, this situation is changing rapidly and dramatically. At the end of December 1997 the percentage figures for cases conducted in Chinese were as follows (the starting date differs from court to court): District Court: 15.76; Lands Tribunal: 58.54; CFI appeals: 22.67; CFI trials: 9.74; Court of Appeal: 7.02. It appears that, very soon, the majority of trials will be heard in Chinese. The Hong Kong Law Reports, however, are not available in Chinese. Simultaneous translation is provided in LegCo, UrbCo, and RegCo, where councillors can use either English or Cantonese, as in the District Boards.

A major development was the decision in 1989 to translate the entire statute book into Chinese and to draft new ordinances and some subsidiary legislation in both languages, with both language versions to be equally authentic. The government committed considerable resources to this project, which is now completed. No decision has yet been taken to translate written judgments of the Hong Kong courts, although some judgments have appeared in Chinese only. It would be impossible, and probably pointless, to provide Chinese versions of decisional law from other common law jurisdictions. Some secondary legal literature in Chinese is beginning to emerge, but legal education will probably continue to be in English only. In 1987–8, an optional course on the use of Chinese in law was introduced into the degree curriculum at the Faculty of Law at the University of Hong Kong. Government policy is that, eventually, any judicial officer will be able to use either or both of the official languages in any proceedings before him as he sees fit, and parties, witnesses, and legal representatives will have a free choice regarding which language to use. When this is fully implemented the constitutional obligation will have been met. It could be some time, however, before the higher appellate courts use Chinese (though some trials in the Court of First Instance have been heard in that language), and perhaps they will do so rarely, for the legal sources of the common law will always be predominantly in English.

THE OMBUDSMAN

The Office of Members of the Executive and Legislative Councils (OMELCO) used to be significant for the political and legal system because it operated as an ombudsman, or 'grievance-settling body'; that is, complaints about the government were investigated on behalf of councillors and, where possible, redress was secured. OMELCO had no statutory access to government records, but it claimed the co-operation of government departments when inquiring into allegations of maladministration, and it undoubtedly served a useful purpose. Grievances which could not be handled efficiently by the Office, or by urban councillors in their wards, or by some other device, might have ended up in the courts, and litigation is usually best avoided where alternatives are available.

But OMELCO was replaced by the Legislative Council Commission in 1994, a body designed partially to promote the independence from government of legislative councillors. Its complaints-hearing role had in 1988 been supplemented (and in practice largely superseded) by a Commissioner for Administrative Complaints, with the duty of investigating complaints by persons claiming to have sustained injustice as a result of maladministration by a government department. 'Maladministration' means 'inefficient, bad, or improper administration' such as delay, discourtesy, and abuse of power. Some types of action, including any exercise of the prerogative of mercy and the grant of honours, and some types of complaint, including those made anonymously or tardily, are excluded. In 1996, the role and powers of the Commissioner were expanded and he is now known as the Ombudsman. He is independent, in the sense that he is statutorily required to act in accordance with his own discretion.

THE DELIVERY OF LEGAL SERVICES

The legal system exists to provide various important services to the community. These services are the jobs best performed by lawyers: they include general counselling, advice as to what the law is and how it can be mobilized in a particular case, the actual task of mobilizing it, participation in the process once the individual's problem has been engaged by the system, and assistance in securing implementation of the result. The degree and distribution of access to these services is a measure of the performance of the legal system — for the law's underlying ideology claims that citizens enjoy equality of access to lawyers and the courts. The study of access can be assisted by a rather hard-headed view of the law, seeing it not in idealistic terms but from the perspective of a consumer. Law is a means of getting things done, of satisfying wants, of providing a special type of product, service, or commodity to be used by clients.

How successful is the Hong Kong legal system in delivering legal services? This question has never been addressed by any sustained inquiry into the organization of the system in its social context. The system was established in the nineteenth century according to a regular colonial model when it was easy to assume that British justice was superior to any other. The rapid influx of Chinese into British Hong Kong encouraged the notion that the measure of certainty, order, and impartiality provided by the colonial government was much to be preferred to the insecurity of arbitrary rule by Chinese officials of the Qing dynasty. Hong Kong was then, much more than now, a place in which to do business, a place for profitable but temporary sojourn before prosperous retirement elsewhere — and so long as the system permitted success in business by the provision of law and order, little else was needed. But conditions in Hong Kong have changed dramatically in this century and particularly since the Second World War. The territory is now the more or less permanent home of much of its population, and there is a consequent need for greater emphasis on the quality of life. One result of the riots in 1966 and 1967 was recognition that social stability demanded improvements in government, and such developments as the establishment of City District Offices and greater security for employees ensued. A number of reforms of the legal profession, such as in effect the abolition of scale fees in conveyancing transactions, have recently been implemented, and perhaps more are to come. In other aspects the legal system has responded to new pressures, but slowly, in a piecemeal, ad hoc fashion: there has been no fundamental rethink of what is required.

Implicit in the foregoing is the simple fact that social change operates in Hong Kong with often bewildering pace: industrialization (or more recently de-industrialization), urbanization, population growth (particularly through immigration from mainland China), the extension of government services and thus the size of government — such factors mean rapid change in the conditions affecting citizens' rights and duties. Political conditions, with the transition to Chinese rule, have affected expectations. Without a carefully considered and well-planned response from the legal system, it is inevitable that the availability and quality of legal services will be crucially affected. It does not seem a useful hypothesis that a system developed in England and in some respects found wanting there can be transplanted with only minor modifications to Hong Kong and yet provide proper legal services to the community.

The following problems, it can be suggested, are some of those that stand in the way of genuine equality of access to legal services:

1. *Recognizing a legal problem* — Many people do not realize that the law can assist them: they are ignorant of what the law is, how it works, and what it can do. The law is thought of as something remote, to be feared and avoided where possible. The paucity of elementary legal education and the absence of neighbourhood law centres, where advice and assistance could be given free or at small cost, ensure that many problems do not receive proper attention.

2. *Finding a lawyer* — Despite rapid expansion of the legal profession, which has accompanied the growth of Hong Kong as a financial centre, there are simply too few lawyers to provide solutions to all the legal problems which arise. Most lawyers serve the commercial community, building up lucrative practices, and defend people accused of crime. But, to borrow a phrase from a former Attorney General, Michael Thomas QC, lawyers are needed not just in the 'green pastures' but at the 'grass roots' as well. Reflecting the type of work most lawyers do is the spatial distribution of their offices: in 1985, over 75 per cent of lawyers' offices were on Hong Kong Island, most of them in Central District; about 13 per cent were in urban Kowloon (Tsim Sha Tsui, Mong Kok, and Yau Ma Tei); and only 9 per cent were in the New Territories (all in the new towns except for just one in Sheung Shui). These statistics have not significantly changed since then. For many people the necessity of travelling long distances and taking time off work in order to see a solicitor means the effort is of dubious value.

3. *Expense* — The legal aid, advice, and assistance schemes are of considerable value in extending access to lawyers and courts. Not all cases of need, however, are covered, and there remain many people for whom legal services are too expensive to contemplate. Fusion of the legal profession would certainly lower costs for some (though not all) legal services in relation to actual or potential litigation. The legal profession has sought to tackle seriously the problems of commission-taking and touting, disreputable practices which add to the cost of law, and its measures are being monitored; if they are unsuccessful it is important that more radical measures be put into effect.

4. *Over-complex law* — The idea of simplifying law and court procedures to encourage people to engage in 'self-help' is initially attractive. In some jurisdictions 'do-it-yourself' divorce and conveyancing kits are available, where the law is so straightforward that citizens can dispense with the services of lawyers. Mediation and other alternative forms of dispute resolution might discourage resort to the courts. The Labour and Small Claims Tribunals do not normally allow lawyers to appear. 'Crimes without victims', such as possessing drugs for personal consumption, could be eliminated, and a thorough-going system of 'no fault' accident compensation introduced, which would render lawyers largely redundant in these areas. Reforms of this kind are inherently controversial, however, and their impact on the total availability of legal services might well

be minimal. Establishment of a Human Rights Commission would assist the public to learn of their rights and lawyers to operate effectively under the Bill of Rights Ordinance. The Equal Opportunities Commission, established in 1996, and perhaps the Privacy Commissioner, could be models for other bodies whose role would include education and publicity, monitoring compliance, research, mediation, and legal assistance.

Much could be done to improve access to law. Civic education at the secondary school level, more lawyers, the creation of law centres, more liberal funding of the Legal Aid Department, law reform in general, codification: some of these are happening already. But the difficulties mentioned above are no doubt not the only ones which impede development of a legal system truly responsive to the demands of those who need legal services. The establishment of a permanent commission, with responsibility for identifying solutions, would be a worthwhile innovation. The ideology of the legal system proclaims the value of the rule of law, yet the rule of law is an objective rather than an accomplished fact. If regular efforts to achieve it are not seen to be made, the ideology risks being dismissed as pure propaganda.

Notes

There are many general accounts of the English legal system which can be referred to for comparative information. See, for example, Phil Harris, *An Introduction to Law* (London: Weidenfeld and Nicholson, 1988, third edition), Marcel Berlins and Clare Dyer, *The Law Machine* (Harmondsworth: Penguin, 1986, second edition), and P. S. Atiyah, *Law and Modern Society* (Oxford and New York: Oxford University Press, 1983). For an introduction to Australia's legal system, see Richard Chisholm and Garth Nettheim, *Understanding Law* (Melbourne, Sydney, Brisbane: Butterworths, 1988, third edition). For Hong Kong, see Albert H. Y. Chen, 'The Legal System' in Joseph Y. S. Cheng (ed.), *Hong Kong in Transition* (Hong Kong: Oxford University Press, 1986), ch. 4; Peter Wesley-Smith, 'The Legal System' in Raymond Wacks (ed.), *The Law in Hong Kong 1969–1989* (Hong Kong: Oxford University Press, 1989), ch. 1; and the legal system chapters in the series of *The Other Hong Kong Report* (Hong Kong: Chinese University Press, 1989–96).

NOTES TO CHAPTER 1

p. 2: Parkinson's First Law: see C. Northcote Parkinson, *The Law* (Boston: Houghton Mifflin Company, 1980). Parkinson has discovered other such laws, for example, the Law of Triviality (the time spent on any item of the agenda will be in inverse proportion to the sum involved), the Law of Delay (delay is the deadliest form of denial), and the Law of the Vacuum (action expands to fill the void created by human failure). For another example of a societal law, see p. 104 (Wesley-Smith's Law).

p. 3: the social functions of law: see Joseph Raz, *The Authority of Law: Essays on Law and Morality* (Oxford: Clarendon Press, 1979), ch. 9.

p. 4: performed by various techniques: see Robert S. Summers, 'The Technique Element in Law' (1971) 59 California L. R. 733, discussed in John H. Farrar and Anthony M. Dugdale, *Introduction to Legal Method* (London: Sweet & Maxwell, 1990, third edition), ch. 2.

p. 4: law and morality: see the classic exchange of views between P. Devlin, *The Enforcement of Morals* (London: Oxford University Press, 1965) and H. L. A. Hart, *Law, Liberty and Morality* (London and Oxford: Oxford University Press, 1963). This topic has generated a voluminous literature.

p. 5: homosexuality and the law in Hong Kong: see H. J. Lethbridge, *Hard Graft in Hong Kong: Scandal, Corruption, the ICAC* (Hong Kong: Oxford University Press, 1985), pp. 196 ff. and 154 ff.

p. 5: law and justice: various conceptions of justice are collected and analysed in F. E. Dowrick, *Justice According to the English Common Lawyers* (London: Butterworths, 1961). See also Roscoe Pound, *An Introduction to the Philosophy of Law* (New Haven and London: Yale University Press, 1954), ch. 3, and Richard A. Wasserstrom, *The Judicial Decision: Toward a Theory of Legal Justification* (Stanford: Stanford University Press, 1961), ch. 5.

p. 8: the legitimacy of law: see essays in Patrick McAuslan and John F. McEldowney (eds.), *Law, Legitimacy and the Constitution* (London: Sweet & Maxwell, 1985).

p. 9: the transfer of sovereignty in 1997: see Yash Ghai, *Hong Kong's New Constitutional Order: The Resumption of Chinese Sovereignty and the Basic Law* (Hong Kong: Hong Kong University Press, 1997).

p. 11: the decision of the Court of Appeal: *HKSAR v. David Ma Wai-kwan* [1997] 2 H.K.C. 315.

NOTES TO CHAPTER 2

p. 12: a legal system: see Marc Galanter, 'Delivering Legality' (1976) 11 Law and Society Review 225, 227.

p. 15: ideology: the classic account of the rule of law is provided by A. V. Dicey, *Introduction to the Study of the Law of the Constitution* (London, Macmillan, 1959, tenth edition), ch. 4. See also Joseph Raz, 'The Rule of Law and its Virtue' (1977) 93 L.Q.R. 195; Lon Fuller, *The Morality of Law* (New Haven and London: Yale University Press, 1964, second edition), ch. 2; F. A. Hayek, *The Constitution of Liberty* (London: Routledge and Kegan Paul, 1960), ch. 14; T. R. S. Allan, 'Legislative Supremacy and the Rule of Law: Democracy and Constitutionalism' (1985) 44 C.L.J. 111; Ronald Dworkin, 'Political Judges and the Rule of Law' in Dworkin, *A Matter of Principle* (Cambridge, Mass., and London: Harvard University Press, 1985), ch. 1; Peter Wesley-Smith, *Constitutional and Administrative Law in Hong Kong* (Hong Kong: Longman, 1994, second edition), pp. 14–19.

p. 19: According to one analysis: H. L. A. Hart, *The Concept of Law* (Oxford: Clarendon Press, 1994, second edition).

NOTES TO CHAPTER 3

The first detailed account of the Hong Kong constitution, now somewhat out of date, was provided by John Rear, 'The Law of the Constitution' in Keith Hopkins (ed.), *Hong Kong: The Industrial Colony* (Hong Kong: Oxford University Press, 1971), ch. 8. See now Peter Wesley-Smith, *Constitutional and Administrative Law in Hong Kong* (above).

p. 20: types of constitution: see the standard texts, such as the following, all called *Constitutional and Administrative Law*: by S. A. de Smith (Harmondsworth: Penguin, 1990, sixth edition); O. Hood Phillips (London: Sweet & Maxwell, 1987, seventh edition), ch. 1; E. C. S. Wade and A. W. Bradley (London: Longman, 1985, tenth edition), ch. 1.

p. 22: conventions: see Geoffrey Marshall, *Constitutional Conventions* (Oxford: Clarendon Press, 1984).

p. 23: rule of law: see notes to Chapter 2.

p. 24: separation of powers: see M. J. C. Vile, *Constitutionalism and the Separation of Powers* (Oxford: Clarendon Press, 1967), pp. 1–20.

p. 24: to a large extent it seems to underpin the Basic Law: see Peter Wesley-Smith, 'The Separation of Powers' in Peter Wesley-Smith (ed.), *Hong Kong's Basic Law: Problems and Prospects* (Hong Kong: Faculty of Law, University of Hong Kong, 1990), pp. 71–84.

NOTES TO CHAPTER 4

See generally Norman Miners, *The Government and Politics of Hong Kong* (Hong Kong: Oxford University Press, 1991, fifth edition, updated 1998).

p. 26: not democratic: see John Rear, 'One Brand of Politics' in Keith Hopkins (ed.), *Hong Kong: The Industrial Colony* (Hong Kong: Oxford University Press, 1971), ch. 3; S. N. G. Davies, 'One Brand of Politics Rekindled' (1977) 7 H.K.L.J. 44.

These sources are no longer directly relevant, but they still provide useful discussions of the concept of democracy in a Hong Kong context.

p. 29: Like the Governor before him: see, for comparative material in relation to the position of the Chief Executive, Sir Kenneth Roberts-Wray, *Commonwealth and Colonial Law* (London: Stevens, 1966), pp. 312–14 and 337–41. The Governor's inability to order a civil servant to act contrary to a duty imposed by the legislature was illustrated by *Re the Hong Kong Hunters' Association Ltd.* [1980] H.K.L.R. 179. See also, regarding the Governor's granting of an amnesty to police officers charged with corruption, Peter Wesley-Smith, Note (1978) 8 H.K.L.J. 241. The principles of law relating to the colonial Governor, discussed in these sources, are just as applicable to the Chief Executive.

p. 32: duty to act fairly: the area of law known as administrative law has, in quite recent times, developed the notion that government officers have no authority to act unfairly. What is fair or unfair depends on all the circumstances, including the legislation under which the officer is purporting to act. See the general textbooks or, for a useful short account, D. C. M. Yardley, *Principles of Administrative Law* (London: Butterworths, 1986, second edition).

p. 33: municipal and rural government: see the legislation which establishes the various institutions and regulates their powers and functions: the Urban Council Ordinance (cap. 101), the Regional Council Ordinance (cap. 385), the Heung Yee Kuk Ordinance (cap. 1097), and the District Boards Ordinance (cap. 366).

p. 35: law-enforcement agencies: see the Police Force Ordinance (cap. 232) and the Independent Commission Against Corruption Ordinance (cap. 204).

NOTES TO CHAPTER 5

p. 37: the common law: see Glanville Williams, *Learning the Law* (London: Stevens, 1982, eleventh edition), ch. 2.

p. 38: the reception of English law: see Peter Wesley-Smith, *The Sources of Hong Kong Law* (Hong Kong: Hong Kong University Press, 1996), part 2.

p. 40: *Gensburger* v. *Gensburger* is reported at [1968] H.K.L.R. 403. This case, and its theoretical consequences, were discussed by John Rear at (1972) 2 H.K.L.J. 115; and see Wesley-Smith, *The Sources of Hong Kong Law* (above), pp. 116–18.

p. 41: bizarre results could yet be envisaged: see ibid. pp. 118–19.

p. 41: *Oceania Manufacturing Co.* v. *Pang Kwong-hon*: reported at [1979] H.K.L.R. 445.

p. 43: injustice or oppression: *Wong Yu-shi (No. 1)* v. *Wong Ying-kuen* [1957] H.K.L.R. 420, 442–3.

p. 43: liberal and imaginatively construed: Lord Denning in *Nyali Ltd.* v. *A.G.* [1956] 1 Q.B. 1, 16–17.

p. 43: succession upon intestacy: *Ho Tsz-tsun* v. *Ho Au-shi* (1915) 10 H.K.L.R. 69. See now the Intestates Estates Ordinance (cap. 73).

p. 43: building contracts: *Lau Yeong-wood* v. *Standard Oil* (1908) 3 H.K.L.R. 53, 59–60.

p. 43: a wife cannot give evidence against her husband in criminal proceedings: *Chan Hing-cheung* v. *R.* [1974] H.K.L.R. 196, 208–12.

p. 43: magistrate granting bail: *Man Kam-fat* (1947) 1 H.K.L.R. 13, 18.

p. 43 the 'reasonable man' in Hong Kong: *Ma Wai-fun* [1962] H.K.L.R. 61.

NOTES TO CHAPTER 6

p. 48: Bill of Rights: see the Hong Kong Bill of Rights Ordinance 1991.

p. 49: limits the territorial reach: see Wesley-Smith, *Constitutional and Administrative Law in Hong Kong* (above), pp. 205–9.

p. 49: subsidiary legislation: see ibid., pp. 215–25; Part V, Interpretation and General Clauses Ordinance (cap. 1). The *ultra vires* doctrine is illustrated by *Wong Pun-cheuk v. Medical Council* [1964] H.K.L.R. 47 and *Lau Ping* [1970] H.K.L.R. 343.

p. 50: common law and equity: on whether English judicial decisions are binding see Chapter 9.

p. 50: Chinese customary law: see Wesley-Smith, *The Sources of Hong Kong Law* (above), ch. 12.

p. 51: both the Chinese Imperial Codes and local customary law: see, e.g., *Re the Estate of Ng Shum (No 2)* [1990] H.K.L.R. 67.

p. 51: land in the New Territories: s. 13, New Territories Ordinance (cap. 97).

p. 51: abolished by various ordinances: see D. M. E. Evans, 'The New Law of Succession in Hong Kong' (1973) 3 H.K.L.J. 7.

p. 53: British officials who maintained custom in the New Territories: see the unpublished paper by Howard Nelson, 'British Land Administration in the New Territories of Hong Kong, and its Effects on Chinese Social Organization' (1969).

p. 53: 'wife' in the Evidence Ordinance: *Chan Hing-cheung* [1974] H.K.L.R. 196.

NOTES TO CHAPTER 7

For an account of how little legal literature there was in the 1970s, see Peter Wesley-Smith, *Legal Literature in Hong Kong* (Hong Kong: Centre of Asian Studies, 1979). A more modern account is in Jill Cottrell, *Legal Research: A Guide for Hong Kong Students* (Hong Kong: Hong Kong University Press, 1997); see also Cottrell's 'The State of Hong Kong's Legal Literature: Law Reports, Legislation, and Current Awareness' (1998) 28 H.K.L.J. 5.

p. 55: the statute book: see Michael J. Downey, 'The Laws of Hong Kong' (1989) 19 H.K.L.J. 147.

p. 58: a loose-leaf edition: see the Laws (Loose-Leaf Publication) Ordinance 1990.

NOTES TO CHAPTER 8

See the following legislation: the Magistrates Ordinance (cap. 227), the Coroners Ordinance (cap. 14), the District Court Ordinance (cap. 336), the High Court Ordinance (cap. 4), the Hong Kong Court of Final Appeal Ordinance (cap. 484), the Small Claims Tribunal Ordinance (cap. 338), the Labour Tribunal Ordinance (cap. 25), and the Lands Tribunal Ordinance (cap. 17).

p. 69: habeas corpus: a writ directed to a person detaining another; it commands that the detainee be brought before the court, where the validity of the detention can be examined. If the detainee is in unlawful custody, the judge can set him free.

p. 72: the Labour Tribunal: see R. A. V. Ribeiro, *The Law and Practice of the Hong Kong Labour Tribunal* (Hong Kong: Centre of Asian Studies, 1978).

NOTES TO CHAPTER 9

There are many accounts, intended for law students, of how decisional law operates. See, for example, David R. Miers and William Twining, *How To Do Things With Rules* (London: Weidenfeld and Nicholson, 1991, third edition); John F. Farrar and Anthony M. Dugdale, *Introduction to Legal Method* (London: Sweet & Maxwell, 1990, third edition), chs. 7 and 8: Michael Zander, *The Law-Making Process*

NOTES

(London: Weidenfeld and Nicholson, 1994, fourth edition), chs. 3, 5, and 6; P. F. Smith and S. H. Bailey, *The Modern English Legal System* (London: Sweet & Maxwell, 1996, third edition), ch. 7. On the doctrine of precedent as it might affect the content of the common law in Hong Kong under Chinese sovereignty, see Peter Wesley-Smith, 'The Common Law in the S.A.R.' in Raymond Wacks (ed.), *Hong Kong, China, and 1997: Essays in Legal Theory* (Hong Kong: Hong Kong University Press, 1993).

p. 76: declaratory theory: see Wesley-Smith, *The Sources of Hong Kong Law* (above), pp. 21–5.

p. 77: the realist theory: ibid., pp. 25–7.

p. 78: analogy from quantum mechanics: the quotation is from John Gribbin, *In Search of Schrodinger's Cat* (London: Corgi, 1985), p. 118.

p. 81: the 'snail-in-the-ginger-beer' case: *Donoghue v. Stevenson* [1932] A.C. 562.

p. 83: financial loss arose from carelessly prepared information: *Hedley Byrne & Co. Ltd. v. Heller* [1964] A.C. 465; negligence by a solicitor: *Midland Bank Ltd. v. Hett, Stubbs & Kemp* [1979] Ch. 384; delinquents escaped from detention: *Home Office v. Dorset Yacht Co. Ltd.* [1970] A.C. 1004.

p. 83: farmer who lawfully sprayed his crops with pesticide: *Tutton v. A.D. Walter Ltd.* [1985] 3 W.L.R. 797.

p. 83: the doctrine of precedent: see Wesley-Smith, *The Sources of Hong Kong Law* (above), chs. 3–5, 11.

p. 84: case on appeal from Hong Kong in 1985: *Tai Hing Cotton Mill Ltd. v. Liu Chong Hing Bank Ltd.* [1985] 3 W.L.R. 317, 331. See also *de Lasala v. de Lasala* [1980] A.C. 546.

p. 86: per incuriam: see Wesley-Smith, *The Sources of Hong Kong Law* (above), pp. 53–63.

NOTES TO CHAPTER 10

p. 87: every ordinance is called a public ordinance: s. 11, Interpretation and General Clauses Ordinance (cap. 1).

p. 87: private bill: see s. 2, Private Bills Ordinance (cap. 69).

p. 87: The process of legislation: see Norman Miners, *The Government and Politics of Hong Kong* (above), pp. 121–6; Standing Orders of the Legislative Council (Appendix II, L.H.K.).

p. 87: private bills may be promoted or adopted: provided they do not have the effect of disposing of or charging any part of Hong Kong's revenue.

p. 89: comes into operation: s. 20, Interpretation and General Clauses Ordinance (cap. 1).

p. 90: subsidiary legislation: s. 3, Interpretation and General Clauses Ordinance. See also Part V of the ordinance.

p. 90: laid on the table of LegCo: s. 34, Interpretation and General Clauses Ordinance.

p. 91: statutory interpretation: a relatively short guide to the subject is provided by Sir Alfred R. N. Cross, *Statutory Interpretation* (London: Butterworths, 1995, third edition).

p. 91: section 19, cap. 1: see Wesley-Smith, *The Sources of Hong Kong Law* (above), ch. 14.

p. 92: literal meaning: *Sussex Peerage Case* (1844) 8 E.R. 1034: *Cheung Ching-man* [1957] H.K.L.R. 500, 503.

p. 92: the duty of the court: the quotation is from *Ng Kam-yuen* [1960] H.K.L.R. 349, 352.

p. 93: in relation to adoption: *Re an Infant* [1962] H.K.L.R. 167.

p. 93: 'golden rule': *River Wear Commissioners* v. *Adamson* (1877) App. Cas. 743.

p. 93: the courts may consult the words of the promoter of the statute: *Pepper* v. *Hart* [1992] 2 W.L.R. 1032.

p. 94: in terms of the 'mischief': *Heydon's Case* (1584) 76 E.R. 637.

p. 94: purposive approach: see, e.g., *Fothergill* v. *Monarch Airlines* [1981] A.C. 251, 278.

p. 95: presumption against strict liability: compare *Mohammed Darais* v. *A.G.* [1976] H.K.L.R. 386 with *Halim Sulman Sharifudin* (1977) 7 H.K.L.J. 378, from which the quotation is taken.

p. 95: presumption against the retrospective operation of statutes: see *Ngai Sau-ying* v. *Henry Chue Kwok-keung (No. 2)* [1982] H.K.L.R. 256, 266.

p. 95: presumption against the exclusion of natural justice: see *Wong Pun-cheuk* v. *Medical Council* [1964] H.K.L.R. 47 and *Lau Ping* [1970] H.K.L.R. 343.

p. 95: authority to cancel a licence: see *Re Tse Cho* [1979] H.K.L.R. 339.

p. 95: presumption against intending inconvenience or unreasonableness: see *Chu Kwok-fai* [1973] H.K.L.R. 107, from which the quotation is taken.

NOTES TO CHAPTER 11

p. 97: the Chief Executive: see Chapter 4. The powers and functions of the Chief Executive are set out in BL48.

p. 97: Emergency Regulations Ordinance: cap. 241.

p. 99: an assured majority in LegCo: from 1976, the official seats were not in fact filled, giving the unofficial members a majority. Not until 1984 did the number of unofficial positions exceed those for official members. See Norman Miners, *The Government and Politics of Hong Kong* (Hong Kong: Oxford University Press, 1986, fourth edition), pp. 123–4.

p. 100: Secretary for Justice: this official is given wide powers in choosing the appropriate charge, the court in which the charge is to be heard, and in bringing a prosecution to an end.

p. 100: the office of Official Solicitor: see the Official Solicitor Ordinance 1991.

p. 100: lawyers: see the (much amended) Legal Practitioners Ordinance (cap. 159).

p. 101: academic training: the Faculty of Law at the University of Hong Kong proposed in 1987 a four-year LLB degree, entry to the programme to be available after one year of sixth form. This did not eventuate, though the Law Society has recently proposed a four-year LLB after two years of sixth form.

p. 103: divided profession: see the final report of the Benson Committee, *Royal Commission on Legal Services* (1979; Cmnd. 7648), ch. 17; Law Society of Hong Kong, *The Future of the Legal Profession in Hong Kong* (1993); Hong Kong Bar Association, *The Future of the Legal Profession in Hong Kong: The Bar's Position Paper* (1994); Peter Wesley-Smith, 'Nineteenth-Century Fusion of the Legal Profession in Hong Kong' (1992) 22 HKLJ 257.

p. 104: a working party chaired by the Chief Justice: see Alison Conner, 'Regulation of Foreign Lawyers in Hong Kong' (1992) 22 HKLJ 132.

p. 106: by delegation in respect of lower levels: see *David Chiu* v. *A.G.* [1992] 2 H.K.L.R. 87 and 'Delegation of Power to Appoint Judicial Officers', Gazette G. N. 457/92.

p. 106: Judicial Officers Recommendation Commission: see the Judicial Officers Recommendation Commission Ordinance (cap. 92).

p. 106: qualifications: see the ordinances regulating the various courts and tribunals.

p. 107: 'constitutional outrage' for judges to receive instructions: this expression was used by Mr Michael Thomas QC in a speech at a public seminar organized by the Hong Kong Affairs Society on 3 June 1984.

p. 108: a judge is middle-aged: Sir Denys Roberts in *Management of Corrections in the Commonwealth* (Hong Kong: Correctional Services Department, 1985), p. 7.

p. 110: Some interesting statistics: see Peter Wesley-Smith, 'The Criminal Courts' in Harold Traver and Mark Gaylord (eds.), *The Criminal Justice System in Hong Kong* (Hong Kong: Hong Kong University Press, 1993).

p. 110: Justices of the Peace: see Justices of the Peace Ordinance (cap. 510).

NOTES TO CHAPTER 12

p. 112: juries: see the Jury Ordinance (cap. 3).

p. 113: legal aid: see the Legal Aid Ordinance (cap. 91) and the Legal Aid in Criminal Cases Rules (cap. 221).

p. 117: the language of the law: see Albert H. Y. Chen, '1997: The Language of the Law in Hong Kong' (1985) 15 H.K.L.J. 19; Official Languages Ordinance (cap. 5).

p. 117: A major development: see Part IIA of the Interpretation and General Clauses Ordinance (cap. 1) and ss. 4–4C of the Official Languages Ordinance (cap. 5).

p. 118: ombudsman: see Ian Scott, 'An Ombudsman for Hong Kong?' South China Morning Post, 27 May 1985, the government's consultative document 'Redress of Grievances' (Hong Kong: Government Printer, 1986), Johannes Chan, 'Hong Kong's Administrative Complaints System' (1996) 26 H.K.L.J. 339, and the Ombudsman Ordinance (cap. 397).

p. 121: not just in the green pastures but at the grass roots: see the speech by the Attorney General at the ceremonial opening of the legal year 1987. Obviously pleased with it, he used the phrase again in a speech at the Chinese University of Hong Kong on 20 February 1987. It is not a particularly apt metaphor, however, since green pastures necessarily contain grass roots, whereas expensive commercial lawyers do not necessarily deal with the legal problems of ordinary working people.

p. 122: establishment of a permanent commission: see Peter Wesley-Smith, 'The Provision of Legal Services in Hong Kong' (1977) 7 H.K.L.R. 289.

Index

ACADEMICS, *see* Legal personnel
Adversarial approach, 7, 14, 67

BARRISTERS, *see* Lawyers
Basic Law, 9–11, 21, 23, 26, 27, 28, 38, 42, 44, 47, 49, 51, 53, 65, 71, 99, 113
Bill of Rights, 48, 115–16, 122

CENTRAL PEOPLE'S GOVERNMENT, 26
Chief Executive, 21, 25, 26, 27–30, 31–2, 47, 49, 50; appoints judicial officers, 106; authority over military, 28; dismissal of, 28; powers and functions of, 28–9; qualifications of, 27; signs bills, 28–9; 87, 89, 90, 97–8; term of office, 28
Chief Secretary for Administration, 30, 31
Chinese Communist Party, 8
Chinese customary law, 4, 38, 50–3; abolition of, 51; administration by British, 51–3; composition of, 51; inapplicable, 53; modifies other law, 53; nature of, 51
Common law, 13, 22, 37–8, 40–2, 50; applicability and modification, 42–4; approaches to statutory interpretation, 92–4; idea of justice, 5–8; judicial precedent, q.v.; meaning of, 37–8; *ratio decidendi* and *obiter dictum*, 79–83; reception from England, 38–42; theories of adjudication, 76–9; *see also* Decisional law
Constitution of Hong Kong, 20–5; abstract (broad), 21–3; ideology, 23–4; rule of law, q.v.; separation of powers, q.v.; simple characteristics, 24–5; written, concrete, 21
Constitution of China, 48
Constitutions, 20–5; broad, 20; codified, 20; concrete, 20; controlled, 25; conventions, 22, 109; narrow, 20; written, 20
Courts and tribunals, 14–15; 21, 65–75; appeals, 73 (chart), 75; coroner, 14, 68; Court of Appeal, 14, 70, 71, 75, 85, 86; Court of Final Appeal, 14, 65, 70–1, 75, 84–5, 86, 105, 108; Court of First Instance, 14, 66, 67, 68, 69–70, 71, 72, 75, 86, 112; District Court, 14, 68–9, 70, 72, 75, 101, 113; House of Lords, 50, 70, 84–5, 86; how to determine which court or tribunal ought to consider a particular matter, 74; Judicial Committee of Privy Council, 50, 70, 84–5, 86, 108; jurisdiction, 65; juvenile court, 68; Labour Tribunal, 14, 72, 75; Lands Tribunal, 72, 75; magistracies, 67–8; original and appellate jurisdiction, 66; other tribunals, 73–5; parties, 66; Small Claims Tribunal, 14, 71–2, 75; summary and indictable offences, 67; superior and inferior, 65–6; terminology, 65–7

DECISIONAL LAW, 76–86; declaratory theory, 39, 76–8; precedent, 83–6; *ratio decidendi* and *obiter dictum*, 79–83; realist theory, 77–8; wavicle theory, 76–9
Declaratory theory, *see* Decisional law
Democracy, 14, 26–7, 35
Department of Justice, 15
District Boards, 26, 35

ENGLISH LAW: Application of English Law Ordinance 1966, 40–4; legislation, 44; practice and procedure, 44; reception of, 39–46; unsuited to Hong Kong, 50–1
Equity, 7, 37–8, 40–2; applicability and modification, 42–4; in Hong Kong, 50; reception from England, 38–42
Executive Council, 15, 21, 29, 30–1, 87–8, 90, 97, 107; appointment, 30; consultation with, 31; functions, 30, 31; ministerial government, 30

FINANCE COMMITTEE, 32
Financial Secretary, 30

GOVERNMENT, 26–36; Chief Executive, q.v.; defined, 26; District Boards, q.v.; executive authority, 29–30; Executive Council, q.v.; Government–LegCo

Committee, 33; 'gubernatorial', 27–30; law-enforcement agencies, 35–6; Legislative Council, q.v.; Legislative Council Commission, 33; municipal and rural, 33–5; police, q.v.; public service, q.v.; Regional Council, q.v.; Urban Council, q.v.; subject to law, 30; whether democratic, 26–7

HEUNG YEE KUK, 34–5
Homosexuality and the law, 5
Hong Kong Law Reform Commission, 5, 87

ICAC, 15, 36
Inland Revenue Board of Review, 14
Institutions, 13–15; courts of justice, q.v.; executive, 15; Executive Council, q.v.; judicial, see Courts of justice; juries, q.v.; legislature, see Legislative Council; Legislative Council, q.v.

JOINT DECLARATION, 9, 70–1
Judges and magistrates, 85–6, 105–10; appointment, 106; conservative, 108; judicial independence, q.v.; localisation, 107; numbers, 105; qualifications, 106–7; statistics, 110
Judicial independence, 25, 107–10; adequate remuneration, 109; appointment, 109; contempt power, 109; convention, 109; dress, 109; immunity of judges, 109; institutional autonomy, 109–10; Judicial Officers Recommendation Commission, q.v.; security of tenure, 108–9
Judicial Officers Recommendation Commission, 29, 100, 106, 108, 109
Judicial precedent, 7, 50, 83–6; consistency and predictability, 86; hierarchy of courts, 73 (chart), 84; horizontal *stare decisis*, 86; House of Lords decisions, 84–5, 86; Judicial Committee decisions, 84–5, 86; NPC Standing Committee interpretations of Basic Law, 84; per incuriam, 86; reference to precedents of other common law jurisdictions, 86; vertical *stare decisis*, 85, 86
Juries, 7, 46, 112–13
Justice, 17, 77, 117; concepts of, 5–8

LANGUAGE OF THE LAW, 59, 117–18
Law reform, 116

Law reporting, 59–63; computerization, 62–3; format of judgment, 61; format of reports, 60; Hong Kong Law Reports, 60–2; in England, 59–60; in Hong Kong, 60–2; summaries of judgments in *Hong Kong Law Journal*, 62
Law, classifications of, 18–19; civil, 19; common law, q.v.; criminal, 19; historical, 2; international, 18; municipal, 18; national, 18; primary, 19; private, 19; procedural, 19; public, 19; regional, 18; secondary, 19; sources, 19, 52; substantive, 19;
Law: Chinese customary, q.v.; common law, q.v.; dependent upon politics, 9; equity, q.v.; functions of, 3–4; ideology, 15–18 (see also Rule of law, Separation of powers); imported law, 37–46; institutions, 13–15; justice and, 5–8; laws previously in force, 38; legal law, 1; legal sources (chart), 52; legislation, q.v.; legitimacy of, 8–9; literary sources, q.v.; made in Hong Kong, 47–53; moral, 2; morality and, 4–5; Murphy's, 2; national laws, 46; Parkinson's, 2; personnel, 15; physical law and, 1; processes, 13; reception of English law, 38–40; religious, 2; rule of law, q.v.; rules and principles, 12–13; rules of etiquette and fashion and, 2; societal, 2; social functions of, 3–4; techniques of, 4; Wesley-Smith's, 104
Lawyers, 15, 100–5; academic training, 101–2; barristers and solicitors, 101, 102–3; foreign, 104–5; fusion, 103–4; numbers, 104; role, 100–1; separate professions, 102–4
Legal Aid Department, 15, 114–15
Legal aid, advice, and assistance, 113–15
Legal education, 15, 101, 104, 120; language, 118
Legal literature, see Literary sources of law
Legal personnel, 97–111; academics, 111; Chief Executive, q.v.; judges and magistrates, q.v.; justices of the peace, 110; lawyers, 100–5; legal officers, 99–100; legislators, 98–9
Legal services, delivery of, 119–22
Legal system: an overview, 12–19; definition of, 12; ideology, 15–18;

institutions, 13–15; personnel, 15; processes, 13; rules and principles, 12–13

Legislation, 12, 76; British, 44–6; creation and interpretation, 87–96; process of, q.v.; delegated legislation, 90–1; limited legislative competence, 47–8; primary, 47–9; statutory interpretation, q.v.; subsidiary, 49–50

Legislative Council, 21, 26, 27, 28–9, 30, 32–3, 47, 48, 88–90, 97, 108; authority, 47–8; 'checks and balances', 29; committees, 32–3; composition, 98–9; elections to, 98–9; 'first LegCo', 98; Government–LegCo Committee, 33; impact of, 32–3; LegCo Commission, 33, 118; process of legislation, q.v.; Provisional LegCo, 11, 22, 29, 33, 98, 99; role of members, 32

Literary sources of law, 54–64; law reporting, q.v.; law lectures for practitioners, 63; primary and secondary, 54–5; secondary materials, 63–4; 'sources', 54–5; statute book, q.v.

MARX, KARL, 2
Morality: and law, 4–5; moral rules, 2

NATIONAL PEOPLE'S CONGRESS, 21, 44, 46, 48, 84, 89

OMBUDSMAN, 118–19
OMELCO, 118

POLICE, 35–6
Precedent, see Judicial precedent
Prerogative, 22, 29
Process of legislation, 87–90; assent, 89; commencement of ordinance, 89; committal, 88; consultation, 88; drafting, 88; method of passing bills, 89; notice of presentation, 88; promulgation, 89; publication of bill, 88; publication of ordinance, 89; recognition of need, 87; reporting to Standing Committee, 89; three readings, 88–9
Public Accounts Committee, 33

Public service, 31–2; organization, 31; Public Service Commission, 29, 31

REGIONAL COUNCIL, 26, 34
Roberts, Sir Denys, 108
Rule of law, 7, 8, 16–18, 23–4, 122; advantageous to individual, 17; antithesis of arbitrary power, 16; capable of guiding behaviour, 17; desirability of, 18; equality, 16–17; exceptions to, 17; formal, rational system, 16; impartial administration, 17; not a rule of law, 17–18; prescriptive, 17–18

SECRETARY FOR JUSTICE, 24, 29, 30, 69, 98, 100, 109, 113
Separation of powers, 24
Solicitors, see Lawyers
Sources of law, 18, 19, 54–5; literary, q.v.; meaning, 54–5; stare decisis, see Judicial precedent; statutes, see Legislation, Statutory interpretation
Sovereignty over Hong Kong, transferred, 9–11
Statute book, 55–9; assessed, 58; looseleaf edition, 58–9; Revised Edition of the Laws Ordinance, 55, 56–8
Statutory interpretation, 91–6; common law approaches, 92–4; constitutional documents, 94; exclusion of natural justice, 95; generally, 91; golden rule, 93, 94; guidelines, 96; intention of legislature, 92; literal rule, 92–3, 94; mischief rule, 94; other principles, 96; presumptions, 94–6; purposive approach, 94; retrospective operation of statutes, 95; statutory rules, 91–2; strict liability offences, 95; unitary approach, 94; unreasonableness, 95–6

TRIBUNALS, see Courts and tribunals
Tung Chee-hwa, 26, 99

UNITED KINGDOM, 20
Urban Council, 26, 33–4